A Daybook for December

In Yellow Springs, Ohio

A Memoir in Nature

and a Handbook for the Month,
Being a Personal Narrative and Synthesis of
Common Events in Nature
between 1981 and 2020
in Southwestern Ohio, with Applications
for the Lower Midwest and Middle Atlantic
Region, Containing Weather Guidelines
and a Variety of Natural Calendars,
Reflections by the Author
and Seasonal Quotations
from Ancient and Modern Writers

By

Bill Felker

A Daybook for the Year in Yellow Springs, Ohio
Volume 12: December

Cover Image from a Watercolor by Libby Rudolf

Copyright 2020 by Bill Felker

Published by The Green Thrush Press
P.O. Box 431, Yellow Springs, Ohio

Printed in the United States of America
Charleston, SC

ISBN: 9781726699518

For Jill

No one suspects the days to be gods.

Ralph Waldo Emerson

Introduction

All my botanical walks, the varied impressions made by the places where I have seen memorable things, the ideas they have aroused in me, all this has left me with impressions which are revived by the sight of the plants I have collected in those places....

Jean-Jacques Rousseau, *Reveries of the Solitary Walker*

The Daybook Format

The format of my notes in this daybook owes more than a little to the almanacs I wrote for the *Yellow Springs News* between 1984 and 2017. The quotations, daily statistics, the weather outlooks, the seasonal calendar, and the daybook journal were and still are part of my regular routine of collecting and organizing impressions about the place in which I live.

Setting: The principal habitat described here is that of Glen Helen, a preserve of woods and glades that lies on the eastern border of the village of Yellow Springs in southwestern Ohio. At its northern edge, the Glen joins with John Bryan State Park to form a corridor about ten miles long, and half a mile wide, along the Little Miami River. The north section of the Glen Helen /John Bryan complex is hilly and heavily wooded, and is the best location for spring wildflowers. The southern portion, "South Glen" as it is usually called, is a combination of open fields, wetlands, and wooded flatlands. Here I found many flowers and grasses of summer and fall. Together, the two Glens and John Bryan Park provide a remarkable cross section of the fauna and flora of the eastern United States.

Other habitats in the daybook journal include my yard with its several small gardens; the village of Yellow Springs itself, a town of 4,000 at the far eastern border of the Dayton suburbs; the Caesar Creek Reservoir, twenty miles south of Yellow Springs and created by the Corps of Engineers in 1976. My trips away from that environment were principally northeast to Chicago, Madison, Wisconsin and northern Minnesota, east to Washington and New York, southeast to the Carolinas and Florida, southwest to Arkansas, Louisiana, and Texas, and occasionally through the Southwest to California and the Northwest, two excursions to Belize in Central America, several to Italy.

Quotations: The passages from ancient and modern writers (and sometimes from my alter egos) which accompany each day's notations are lessons from my readings, as well as from distant seminary and university training, here put to work in service of the reconstruction of my sense of time and space. They are a collection of reminders, hopes, and promises for me that I find implicit in the seasons. They have also become a kind of a cosmological scrapbook for me, as well as the philosophical underpinning of this narrative.

Astronomical Data: The *Daybook* includes approximate dates for astronomical events, such as star positions, meteor showers, solstice, equinox, perihelion (the sun's position closest to earth), and aphelion (the sun's position farthest from Earth).

I have included the sunrise and sunset for Yellow Springs as a general guide to the progression of the year in this location, but those statistics also reflect trends that are world wide, if more rapid in some places and slower in others. All times mentioned in the Daybook are given in Eastern Standard Time.

Even though the day's length is almost never exactly the same from one town to the next, a minute gained or lost in Yellow Springs is often a minute lost or gained elsewhere, and the Yellow Springs numbers can be used as a simple way of watching the lengthening or shortening of the days, and, therefore, of watching the turn of the planet. For those who wish to keep track of the sun themselves in their own location, abundant sources are now available for this information in local and national media.

Average Temperatures: Average temperatures in

Yellow Springs are also part of each day's entry. Since the rise and fall of temperatures in other parts of the North America, even though they may start from colder or warmer readings, keep pace with the temperatures here, the highs and lows in Yellow Springs are, like solar statistics, helpful indicators of the steady progress of the year throughout most of the states along the 40th Parallel east of the Mississippi.

Weather: My daily, weekly and monthly weather summaries have been distilled from over thirty years of observations. They are descriptions of the local weather history I have kept in order to track the gradual change in temperatures, precipitation and cloud cover through the year I have also used them in order to try to identify particular characteristics of each day. They are not meant to be predictions.

Although my interest in the Yellow Springs microclimate at first seemed too narrow to be of use to those who lived outside the area, I began to modify it to meet the needs of a number of regional and national farm publications for which I started writing in the mid 1980s. And so, while the summaries are based on my records in southwestern Ohio, they can be and have been used, with interpretation and interpolation, throughout the Lower Midwest , the Middle Atlantic States and the East.

The Natural Calendar: In this section, I note the progress of foliage and floral changes, farm and garden practices, migration times for common birds, and peak periods of insect activity. Some of these notes are second hand; I'm a sky watcher, but not an astronomer, and I rely on the government's astronomical data and a few other references for much of my information about the stars and the sun. I am also a complete amateur at bird watching, and most of the migration dates used in the seasonal calendar come from published sources. And even though I keep close track of the farm year, the percentages listed for planting and harvesting are interpretations of averages supplied by the state's weekly crop reports.

3

Daybook Entries: The journal entries in the daybook section provide the raw material from which I wrote the Natural Calendar digests. The daybook section is a collection of observations made from the window of my car and from my walks in Glen Helen, in parks and wildlife areas within a few miles of my home, and on occasional trips. It is a record that anyone with a few guidebooks could make, and it includes just a small number of the natural markers that anyone might discover.

When I began to take notes about the world around me, I found that there were few descriptions of actual events in nature available for southwestern Ohio. There was no roadmap for the course of the year. My daily observations, as narrow and incomplete as they were, were especially significant to me since I had found no other narrative of the days, no other depiction of what was actually occurring around me. In time, the world came into focus with each particle I named. I saw concretely that time and space were the sum of their parts.

As my notes for each day accumulated, I could see the wide variation of events that occurred from year to year; at the same time, I saw a unity in this syncopation from which I could identify numerous sub-seasons and with which I could understand better the kind of habitat in which I was living and, consequently, myself. When I paged through the journal entries for each day, I was drawn back to the space in which they were made. I browsed and imagined, returned to the journey.

Companions: Many friends, acquaintances and family members have contributed their observations to the daybook, and their participation has taught me that my private seasons are also community seasons, and that all of our experiences together help to lay the foundation for a rich, local consciousness of natural history.

The Month of December
December Averages: 1981 through 2020
Normal December Average Temperature: 31.2

Year	Average
1981	29.7
1982	39.6
1983	21.9
1984	38.1
1985	23.8
1986	32.8
1987	35.2
1988	30.9
1989	19.0
1990	36.3
1991	34.6
1992	33.0
1993	31.1
1994	37.6
1995	26.5
1996	35.5
1997	33.1
1998	37.0
1999	33.3
2000	20.6
2001	37.2
2002	30.7
2003	33.0
2004	30.7
2005	26.4
2006	38.0
2007	32.7
2008	30.7
2009	30.7
2010	25.1
2011	36.4
2012	38.4
2013	32.6
2014	35.3
2015	43.7
2016	30.3
2017	28.8
2018	36.8
2019	38.0
2020	35.0

December 1st
The 335th Day of the Year

The trumpet of a prophecy! O Wind,
If Winter comes, can Spring be far behind?

Percy Bysshe Shelly

Sunrise/set: 7:37/5:11
Day's Length: 9 hours 34 minutes
Average High/Low: 44/29
Average Temperature: 36
Record High: 67 – 1970
Record Low: 4 – 1964

The Daily Weather

Chances of a mild or warm day improve by 40 percent over yesterday's chances, making this the December day most likely to bring temperatures above 50 degrees (there is a 45 percent chance of that). Highs are in the 40s fifteen percent of the time, in the 30s twenty percent, in the 20s twenty percent. The sun shines seven years out of ten. Rain falls an average of one year in five. Snow comes once in a decade. Early Winter, a pivotal time of decisive cold, is likely to arrive within the next few days, no later than the 8th. The major snow season begins in the Lower Midwest on December 1, typically lasting thirteen to fourteen weeks, ending in the middle of March.

The Week Ahead

Average highs fall three degrees into the lower 40s this week, and typical lows decline to the middle 20s. The first December cold front usually arrives between the 1st and the 3rd, bringing a 40 percent chance of rain or snow on the 2nd and 3rd. The 4th and 5th are dry two years in three; the 6th, however, usually anticipates the second high pressure system of the month and is wet half the days in my record. Afternoon highs do reach the 60s this week of the year, but only five percent of the time. Odds are far better for chilly afternoons in the 30s and 40s and lows well below freezing. December 1st is usually the brightest day of the week, with a 60 percent chance of sun; on the other days of this period, odds are better than 50/50 for clouds.

The December Outlook

Average high temperatures fall from the middle 40s on the first of the month down to the middle 30s on the 31st. Typical lows move from the upper 20s to the lower 20s. Most Decembers bring one or two days above 60, and four days in the 50s, those temperatures frequently recorded before the arrival of Early Winter (around December 8th). The remaining afternoons reach into the 40s an average of seven times, into the 30s thirteen times, finding the 20s three times, and stay in the teens or lower on three occasions.

A morning or two below zero is experienced three years in ten. The period most likely to produce such lows is December 18th through the 26th. The coldest December days, those with better than a 35 percent chance of temperatures in the 20s or below, are the 17th, 18th, 19th, 25th, and 26th. The warmest days, those with a 25 percent or better chance of producing highs in the 60s or 50s, are the 1st, 2nd, 3rd, 7th, 10th, 12th, and 29th.

Skies are completely cloudy on about 12 December days. They are partly cloudy on 15 days, completely cloudless on only four. The average amount of sunshine available this month is 37 percent, the lowest average of the Yellow Springs and Midwestern year.

The darkest December days, those with better than a 60 percent chance of totally overcast conditions, are the 2nd, 3rd, 5th, 6th, 7th, 8th, 11th, 15th, 18th, 19th, 21st, 23rd, 26th, 27th, 28th, 29th, and 31st. The sunniest days, those with more than a 60 percent chance of at least partly cloudy conditions, are the 9th, 14th, 22nd, and the 25th.

A typical December in Yellow Springs brings a little more than two and a half inches of precipitation - included in which are an average of five and a half inches of snow (one inch of snow equals approximately .05 of an inch of water).

The wettest days of the twelfth month, those with more than a 40 percent chance of precipitation, are the 6th, 8th, 10th, 15th, 17th, 19th, 20th, 21st, 22nd, 24th, 30th, and 31st. Rainy days usually outnumber snowy days by about two to one. The days with the least precipitation (just a 20 percent chance): the 1st, 4th, 11th, 16th, and 26th.

Autumncount and Wintercount

The final front of Late Fall typically arrives around December 3rd. After that, the chances of chillier weather increase, and winter arrives on the 8th with the first of its 16 major cold fronts.

December 3: The warmest days of December often take place just before the arrival of this front. As the weather system approaches, rain or snow occurs about one year out of two. Once the December 3rd cold wave comes through, however, dry weather is the rule for the next two days. Now average temperatures are falling at the rate of one degree every two days in most states, and lows almost always fall below freezing above the Mason-Dixon line. By the 6th, the wind shifts to the south and the skies darken in anticipation of the first major high of Early Winter.

December 8: This wave of high pressure is typically the first severe system of Early Winter, and a secondary front often reinforces the chill between the 11th and the 13th. Completely overcast skies dominate more than half the days, and precipitation should be expected as the cold waves approach. The days immediately following the front are typically sunny, and the 10th and 12th often bring warmer conditions. Severe weather with below-zero temperatures and highs only in the teens is still relatively rare below the northern tier of states, but the December 8th front initiates the sixteen-week period during which most snow falls within the borders of the United States.

December 15: The strongest cold wave so far in the season typically moves across the nation between the 15th and the 17th. Some of the coldest December days follow this front. One of the most bitter is the 19th, with a solid chance of highs only in the teens as far south as Cincinnati. The first significant bout of below-zero temperatures in weather history also occurs after this front, and double-digit below-zero temperatures enter the realm of possibility in over half the states. The strength of the December 15th high-pressure system is also associated with higher-than-average precipitation both before and after its arrival.

December 20: The December 20th high-pressure wave is the first of two "white-Christmas" fronts. It is often a relatively mild system, but it has about a 40 percent chance of producing snow in the East and Midwest. Travel is typically favored after the arrival of this front but before the general meteorological disturbances of the 24th.

December 25: The Christmas front is usually a potent one; it brings snow about half the time to the upper half of the nation, and its temperatures are brisk. With the cold comes sun, and the 25th and 26th are historically some of the brightest days of December. It is not unusual for the 27th to initiate a slight warming trend; as the New Year's weather system approaches, however, the sky usually grows cloudy, making the 28th one of the year's gloomiest days.

December 31: The New Year's front often brings wind, sleet or snow. A 50 percent chance of precipitation begins on the 30th and continues through the 31st, but relatively mild weather accompanies the moisture. After this weather system moves to the east, however, the chill of middle winter grips the nation for the next six to twelve weeks.

December Phenology
When the last milkweed seeds scatter along the roadsides, then sunset is the earliest of the year.

When you hear high-pitched honking above you in the night, get up and search the dark sky for sandhill cranes moving south.

When sandhill cranes leave the Midwest, then brown pelicans are nesting along the Gulf of Mexico and larch trees are turning color in Maine.

When the second flowering of forsythia has ended, then gull migrations are finished, too – which completes all major bird migration activity through the nation's midsection for the year. That is the time to prune fruit-bearing bushes in the Lower Midwest and Mid-Atlantic region.

When harvest is complete in the fields, fertilize with organic matter, phosphorus and potassium to reduce soil compaction.

When Early Winter arrives after the moon is new, then sow your first bedding plants for spring; order legume seed for next year's winter pastures; schedule frost seeding for January and February;

order sunflower, beet, Jerusalem artichoke, pumpkin, comfrey, carrot, kale and turnip seeds for livestock.

When crocus and snowdrop foliage pushes up through the mulch, then the first pussy willows will be cracking, and mistletoe will be visible high in the branches of Mississippi woodlots (after the high canopy dissolves).

When the yellow leaves of the New England aster fall, then the pear leaves and the beech leaves (the last holdouts of the canopy) will soon be falling, too.

When beech leaves have all come down in the North, then mangoes are in full bloom throughout southern Florida, and Florida grapefruit will soon be ripe.

When the very last leaves have been taken from all the trees in the Ohio Valley, then ducks have completed migration and below-zero lows remain a possibility until a month after aconites and snowdrops bloom.

When great flocks of crows gather for the winter, then earliest spring is only ten weeks away, and red squirrels get white tufts on their ears.

Key to the Nation's Weather

The typical December temperature, the average of the high of 39 and the low of 26, at median elevations along the 40th Parallel is 32 degrees. Using the following chart based on weather statistics from around the country, a person can estimate the approximate temperatures in other locations. For example, with the average of the 40th Parallel as the base of "32," you can estimate normal temperatures in Minneapolis by subtracting 13 degrees from the 32 degrees (32 − 13 = 19). Or add ten degrees to find out the likely conditions in Seattle during the month.

Fairbanks AK	-39
Minneapolis MN	-13
Des Moines IA	-6
Portland, ME	-5
Detroit MI	-3
Chicago IL	-2
AVERAGE ALONG 40TH PARALLEL	32
New York NY	+3
St. Louis MO	+3

Washington, D.C.	+5
Seattle WA	+10
Dallas TX	+15
New Orleans LA	+24
Miami FL	+37

The Natural Calendar

December 1 is a major point in the progress of the solar year, and the texture of that day's composite includes markers that take Yellow Springs a little farther into winter. At this date, the years in which the village pear trees are completely bare become more frequent, and intrusions of bitter weather become more common. The high-pressure systems that arrive from the west leave deeper frost and flurries.

Milder years may keep second-bloom forsythia and witch hazel flowers open, force snowdrops and crocus foliage to push through the mulch, but in colder years, frames of ice appear more frequently along the riverbanks and on my pond. The color of fallen leaves becomes darker from rains and from freezing and thawing. Unlike during the past century, turkey vultures remain in the area, overwintering like the small flocks of local robins that call from the undergrowth. In another recent change, villagers sometimes hear sandhill cranes that are following what may be a slightly altered flyway to the South.

Daybook

1983: Most all the seeds are gone from the milkweed pods; just a few wisps of down cling to their shells. Despite the cold, rain and flurries, a few forsythia leaves hang on. All Osage and mock orange have fallen.

1986: Next to the shed, a huge pokeweed stem, hollow, brown, fallen, exploded from the cold last night.

1988: I went out through the dead goldenrod, past my fishing hole, to the middle prairie. I sat by rose hips and listened to the wind until the sun went down behind the dark oaks on the west ridge.

1989: A cardinal sang off and on all day. Pears two-thirds gone downtown.

1990: All pear leaves finally down in the village.

1991: Lettuce and spinach, covered with straw, are still edible in the garden. Carrots are still firm. Kale and collards are still providing greens. Garlic shoots are strong and green. A few mums are still alive, provided scattered color by the bird feeder.

1996: Pear leaves still not gone. The Dayton Street beech holds at maybe half, leaves rust-brown. Crows in the yard this morning, also seen along Dayton Street on the way home from church. A few yellow forsythia blooming by the front fence.

1997: One witch hazel done blooming, one full bloom on Dayton Street.

1999: Deep freeze this morning, temperatures in the teens, pond has ice for the second morning in a row, the first two ice mornings of the winter. Pear trees are lit up at night with Christmas lights, but they still keep maybe a fourth of their brown foliage. The street and sidewalks, though, are covered with their burnished leaves.

2003: A cardinal was singing at 7:30 this morning when I took the garbage outside. Walking Bella, I saw forsythia flowers in bloom low to the ground by the front fence. At the covered bridge in the late afternoon, the river was high but clear from the weekend's rain and snow. All but a few honeysuckle berries had disappeared. A flock of robins fluttered in a white sycamore. A pileated woodpecker flew by. The half moon lay in the bright blue eastern sky. Downtown, almost all the yellow pear leaves had fallen.

2007: Blustery, clouding up, storm moving in, snow and ice in Chicago and the Plains, dire predictions for the East. I build up the fire and hunker down.

2008: Wind and flurries. The alley was quiet this morning, no more robins clucking, no starlings whistling. Barometer slowly rising after yesterday's dip below 29.30. In the backyard, a kaleidoscope of dark, fallen autumn colors, has been dulled further by yesterday's rain. I will measure the progress of the new year in their changes. The decay of the Osage fruit through the months ahead will also help me time the winter.

2009: Ice on the puddles in the alley this morning, starlings whistling. Regrowth on the hydrangeas burned by the frost. I noticed that the witch hazel leaves, all brown and curled for at least a month, have not fallen yet. The last Osage leaves on the east side of the tree hang on. Jeanie and Chris report a large flock of vultures in the trees along Corey Street at about 8:00 a.m.

2010: Light snow all day long, the first wintry day so far since spring. In the greenhouse, all the Christmas cacti are in full bloom.

2011: Cold in the low 20s and clear this morning, the pond frozen over for the first time (first snow two days ago), crows at 7:20 sharp. At the post office, Ed Oxley showed me a photo of one snowdrop flower blooming on his property north of town. Nick Boutis reported sandhill cranes this afternoon, about fifty of them "blaring out their gargling whistle."

2012: When I turned on the light near the wood stove this morning, I saw three camel crickets on the brick wall. They have been encroaching more and more this autumn, haunting the cat box, getting caught in traps I have set for moths in the pantry. Crows at 7:48, a soft start to the day. I weeded a little near the trellis before I went to work, the ground moist and giving. In the east garden, crocus and snowdrop foliage is up half an inch. The new hyacinths I planted have started coming up in the north garden. Record warmth across the Southwest, more records expected in the Great Plains tomorrow, record rains in California.

2013: Crows at 7:25 this mild, cloudy morning, robins peeping, starlings whistling in the distance.

2015: Mild 50 degrees, haze, mare's tails: Inventory after a mild November: Fish still rise for food; honeysuckle leaves pale and maybe two-thirds gone; forsythia leaves mostly down, remnants purple brown like the oakleaf hydrangea's; foliage returning: creeping Charley, garlic mustard, chickweed, bittercress, waterleaf, a few lily sprouts, dock, henbit, celandine, spiderwort; rose leaves deep violet green; lush Shasta daisy leaves; buds on the tips of the Endless Summer hydrangea; the small daisies that I planted from seed late in the summer still have a few flowers.

2016: At the Indian Mound, bright hepatica foliage uncovered as Jeff and I walked through the groundcover of fallen maple leaves. In Jill's side yard, the last red leaves of her burning bush and Japanese maple came down.

2018: Hard rain and mild today, barometer quite low, near 29.50. Neysa sent a photograph of the first major leafturn in the hills around Fontanelli in Italy.

2019: Sunny and mild today, sky robin's egg blue. Cardinal before dawn. Robins peeping throughout the neighborhood all morning. The remaining honeysuckle foliage glows yellow-green, and the day feels like spring.

2020: Flurries early after yesterday's three inch snowfall. Wind and cold 20s throughout the day, bamboo leaning hard from the wet snow, a wave of late honeysuckle berries dropping to the sidewalk. Full moon on the 30th brought an end to this November's mild run.

Shadows on snow look blue. The skier,
Exultant at the summit, sees his poles
elongate toward the valley: thus

each blade of grass projects another
opposite the sun, and in marshes
the mesh is infinite....

John Updike, from "Penumbrae"

December 2nd
The 336th Day of the Year

No one suspects the days to be gods.

Ralph Waldo Emerson

Sunrise/set: 7:38/5:10
Day's Length: 9 hours 32 minutes
Average High/Low: 44/28
Average Temperature: 36
Record High: 72 - 1982
Record Low: 1 – 1886

The Daily Weather

High temperatures are in the 60s or 70s five percent of the time, reach the 50s twenty-five percent of the days, are in the 40s twenty percent, in the 30s thirty percent, are in the 20s fifteen percent, and in the teens five percent. Lows drop below freezing 80 percent of the nights. Precipitation: one day in three, with the odds even for rain or snow.

The Natural Calendar

When sunset reaches its earliest time of the year, the brittle leaves of the pear trees fall. This is the time during which the second bloom of forsythia flowers typically ends, when witch hazel blossoms wither, and the last of the golden beeches, the willows, Osage and oaks come down. The corn and soybean harvests are usually complete all around the county by this date, and development of winter wheat slows in the cold. New garlic shoots are firm and green, but they've stopped growing and remain at their middle-autumn height. The Christmas tree harvest is at its peak, and the last poinsettias have come north.

South-window tomatoes sown in August could be ripening as December arrives. Marigolds, zinnias, impatiens and other bedding plants saved from a hard freeze may still be in flower. The first buds have formed on mother-of-millions. The greenhouse hibiscus blooms, opening before dawn, fading and falling by three in the afternoon.

Poinsettias, placed in the dark about seventeen hours a day through the autumn, should be turning red. In much of the nation, the Season of Earliest Sunset Time starts in the first days of December and continues to midmonth.

Daybook

1982: 70 degrees, sky pale turquoise: Grass snake in the sun by the river. Sounds of squirrels, chickadees, sparrows, starlings, doves, and downy woodpeckers fill the woods. Catnip grows back along High Street. In South Glen: thistle, moneywort, chickweed, wild geranium, leafcup, purple deadnettle, yarrow. At the far fence line, where the woods ends, thistles are stronger, their bright leaves in clusters hugging the ground. Japanese honeysuckle still November green at home.

1984: Reports of hepatica blooming in the warm late autumn.

1988: First paperwhites, started November 22, bloomed today.

1990: Early Winter comes in about this time every year. The percent of mild days falls sharply on my graph around November 28th. Then the two high-pressure systems that come through during the first week of December usually make an end to Late Fall. The last Osage leaves fell overnight. More raking to be done. In the garden, lettuce is still crisp and sweet. Geese flew over in the dark, 5:45 p.m.

1992: Today, the barometer is low, 29.65, the first storm of Early Winter coming in this afternoon. Reading the daybook, comfort in the circle of years, memories tempering and coloring this gray weather now.

1995: The last woolly-bear caterpillars mark one of the many borders of autumn, like the silver maple, pear and beech leaves falling, the arrival of the crows west of Springfield, new growth on the spruce, the flowering of witch hazel, the first snow.

Driving south to Hillsboro on December 2nd, I watched for woolly-bears crossing the road. The sun was bright; it made the wheat fields and pastures glow. The road surface was warm, perfect for caterpillars. They had been out, after weeks of cold, when I came home from Wilberforce on November 20th, three orange and black ones moving across the pavement in the mild afternoon. That was the latest I'd noticed them since beginning to travel Wilberforce-Clifton and Grinnell Roads in 1978. I thought maybe they'd appear again, but the end of November must normally be the outside limit of their activity.

1999: The yellow leaves of the New England aster fall quickly now, the tufted seed heads grow more prominent.

2000: Yucca stalks down this morning, toppled from the weight of the last night's snow.

2001: After a warm November, in soft rain, the grass outside my door is lush and bright, the last Osage leaves golden above the shed. Along the west wall of the house, Shasta daisies are still in bloom. Wild onions are getting lanky, motherwort is bushy, one Queen Anne's lace plant has grown back two-feet tall.

Inside the garden: fresh rosemary, thyme, oregano, fat chard still good for picking. Strawberry leaves are turning red and orange. Dry pumpkin-brown heads of marigold quiver in the wind. By the pond: blush on the wild geranium. By the front door, *lamium purpureum*, dead nettle, full of new growth and purple flowers, dusky forsythia still blocking the street, pink azalea leaves forecasting their spring blossoms.

New chickweed under the rhododendrons, new clover, two new dandelions, henbit deep summer green. Under the apple tree, one wild strawberry flower. To one side of the woodpile, very late blue forget-me-nots. Along the north hedge, orange euonymus berries pushing out from their white pods, late honeysuckle berries, strong sweet William growth, tawny leaves of the goosefoot, feathery achillea returning, butterfly bush and comfrey, dock, garlic mustard all vigorous, two deep yellow roses surrounded by mint, three pale violet sweet rocket flowers nestling against the old stone wall.

2002: Honeysuckle leaves shriveled from the frost, but the Japanese honeysuckle vine still provides some privacy for the windows along the east garden.

2003: Starlings chatter in the morning under the bright sun. At about 11:00, Rick Donahoe called to tell me he had just seen a flock of maybe a hundred cranes honking and flying over his house on Wright Street. "They were going straight south," he said. Sand-hill cranes? Maybe blue herons? Rick didn't think they were herons. "I've seen cranes out West," he told me. "These were like cranes." I saw Phil Hawke downtown a little later. "Sure," he said, "they're cranes. They couldn't be anything else."

2005: Cold and blustery this morning. At South Glen, seven mallards were swimming up and down in the Little Miami River. At the corner of Hyde and Grinnell, scores of Osage fruits, all weathered from chartreuse to yellow-brown, were spread out in the grass, each ball covered with a hat of snow. The subfreezing temperatures of the past weeks have put an end to almost every leaf in the woods.

2008: Light snow and low in the 20s this morning, full Early Winter. One robin heard in the alley, but no other sound. The bittersweet berries have emerged all the way from their hulls; the winterberries are all pushing out.

2009: Oakleaf hydrangea leaves have started to fall. No frost this morning, yesterday's cirrus have become gray altostratus, rain tonight.

2010: Northern Europe is covered with an early cold wave, and Great Britain is covered with snow.

2011: Crows at 7:20 this morning. Soft, sunny day, high close to 50.

2013: Midmorning: Tom called from Dayton Street to say he had seen three Eastern bluebirds (two males and one female) at his feeder.

2015: Robin whinnies and peeps in a foggy morning.

2016: The pear leaves, so rich orange-gold-burnished red and brown, are collapsing throughout town. Ed Oxley sent a photo, taken today, of what appears to be a painted lady butterfly on his fence.

2018. Clear sky, half Moon and Venus in the east at dawn, windy, warm high 50s today. Geese fly back and forth at Ellis Pond. The oaks near the pond still hold their leaves, brown and twisted. The cypress trees keep a thin spread of rusty brown. A small flock of blue jays were clustering in the woodlot near the water. Along the bike path: pods of bittersweet. The koi fed slowly in my pond, moving close together, looking up at me. On the way to Delaware, Ohio with Jill: three small murmurations of starlings, one flock of crows.

2020: Last night's cold in the 20s brought down the last of the Osage leaves, and the forsythia hedge is thinning quickly.

When one pays close attention to the present, there is great pleasure in awareness of small things.

Peter Matthiessen

But let the months go round, a few short months,
And all shall be restored. These naked shoots
Barren as lances, among which the wind
Makes wintry music, sighing as it goes,
Shall put their graceful foliage on again,
And more aspiring and with ampler spread
Shall boast new charms, and more than they have lost.

William Cowper

Sunrise/set: 7:39/5:10
Day's Length: 9 hours 31 minutes
Average High/Low: 43/28
Average Temperature: 36
Record High 71 – 1982
Record Low: 0 – 1929

The Daily Weather

Chances of highs in the 70s are five percent, of 60s ten percent, of 50s fifteen percent, of 40s ten percent, of 30s fifty percent, of 20s ten percent. Skies are cloudy almost two-thirds of the time; rain falls one year in three, snow less than once in a decade. This morning is the first day since March 9th that carries a five percent chance of the temperature to drop to zero or below in the Lower Midwest.

The Natural Calendar

A warm November and early December create a benign cradle for the resurgence of Second Spring. Lawns grow back, often long and thick beneath the fallen leaves. Winter grain, destined for harvest in June, sprouts to turn fields glowing green. The skunk cabbage of March rises below the stairs to the Nature Center and beyond the Covered Bridge.

In fields and woods, garlic mustard, sweet Cicely, celandine, parsnips, sweet rocket, ragwort, dock, hemlock, stinging nettle and chickweed add foliage. Protected by the stable temperature of creeks and rivers, watercress brightens.

Lamium ground cover recovers in dooryards. The latest roses bloom. Pachysandra, its buds formed in May, waits for a warm February. Mint and thyme, rosemary, parsley and verbena are fresh in the garden. New spinach and chard are sweet and tender. Comfrey is fat. Creeping Charlie spreads around them.

Remnants of Middle Summer add to the impression of renewal, pansies or nasturtiums or even petunias, spared from frost, keeping their blossoms. Violets and dandelions sometimes flower on the Antioch lawn. Yellowing honeysuckle glows like April forsythia along the bike path.

In the greenhouse, jade trees and aloe sometimes flower. In south windows, Christmas cacti are open. Paperwhite and amaryllis bulbs extend their stalks for solstice.

Cardinals sometime sing as early as 7:00, their time in earliest spring. Late or overwintering robins call in short bursts or whinnies. Houseflies sometimes hatch in the warmest days. Small moths appear at porch lights. The hardiest crickets still sing for each other in the dark.

Daybook

1980: The first cold front of Early Winter came in today after yesterday's wind and flurries.

1981: Today the composition of Early Winter seems plain and distinct. The absence of migratory birds magnifies the rattle of the downy woodpecker and the calling of the crows. Nothing is concealed by foliage. The natural year is complete and therefore finite and countable. Now there's enough time to look at everything. I can list remnants at leisure. I can rebuild the summer and document spring's progress with simple, reassuring measurements.

My friend Cajuvian always told me that tallying pieces the seasons was all anyone could do. "There isn't really any transcendence," he said. "The excitement and promise of the middle of the year seem to offer a covenant with eternity. But really there's nothing to that promise except a few dried berries, shells, and bare branches." This afternoon was quiet and cold. The black centers of the empty milkweed pods faced the sun. Thistle and garlic mustard, still green, clustered close to the ground. A sparrow hawk was back; it watched the pasture from the barbed wire. Mike Tripplett said that the hawks come to Ohio when the snow gets deep in the north, and the mice are safe under the frozen cover. Here, the fields are still accessible.

There were ducks on the river, no ice yet, even along the sloughs. Osage fruits were open, shredded by the squirrels. The seed heads of ironweed were pale and soft, their stalks hung with love vine by the swamp. Gnats swarmed out of the wind. I saw a black-capped chickadee, a flicker, four titmice, three silent cardinals, white sycamores, some orange honeysuckle berries still left, red rose hips, broken, dark angelica. Doves scattered when I walked through the goldenrod. Skunk cabbage was up at the swamp past the covered bridge.

Tonight, the sun went down at its earliest time of the year. Orion was in the east after supper, the Pleiades overhead, red Taurus between them. The Northern Cross was setting over Dayton. Sirius came up an hour before midnight.

1982: The high reached a record 71 today. My charts give December 6th as the latest date in the past century for an afternoon above 70. The next possible date after the 6th is January 21st.

1988: Sun, wind, 50 degrees, not a single cloud. Everything seemed so transparent and focused today in the brightness. The crisp air made the trees and plants stand out – or else it sharpened my eye. The rivers were down and clear as I've ever seen it. There were dozens of carp and suckers in schools at Far Hole, but they wouldn't take dough balls or worms. The pasture at Middle Prairie was full of spring growth, green with asters, mullein, clover, chickweed, purple deadnettle, dandelions (one even blooming), and winter cress. One grasshopper found, and I heard two cardinals calling back and forth, and then a mocking bird.

1990: Early Winter arrives on schedule tonight after wind all day and snow bursts.

2001: A cardinal sang outside the back door at 7:15 this morning.

2004: Although most of the pear leaves have fallen in Yellow Springs, many pears still have all their foliage in Dayton.

2008: Mild south wind this morning and dropping barometer. Rain forecast for tonight, snow tomorrow. A tufted titmouse heard this morning in the alley. Juncos seen yesterday at the back feeder. Most of the lilac and forsythia leaves are down. Only the Japanese honeysuckle leaves and the bamboo remain green. Endless summer hydrangea flowers are all pale tan. All remnants of the hostas have dissolved into the garden mulch. Artichoke leaves twisted and stiff. The cold and the dusting of snow have stripped the variety of colors from the Osage and mock orange leaves on the ground in the back yard. Some Osage fruit is developing blackish patches. This is a time of deeper browning, a further settling of autumn's fibers.

2009: Rain and cold as high-pressure approaches. Crows at 7:30, buzzards, about 30 or 40, Jeanie says, by the bike path this morning. Cathy writes from Vermont about panic that the weather has been so warm, the snow machine people trying to drum up business.

2010: I planted two flowering cabbages today in the East garden, uncovering a handful of crocus bulbs that were already growing out toward the surface of the ground, their white stalks soft and brittle, easily snapping off as I moved the dirt.

2011: Crows at 7:20 a.m. once again. One dandelion flowering in the alley. In Kettering, lawns full of dandelion seed heads, evidence a full resurgence of Second Spring throughout November.

2012: The morning was foggy and mild. I pulled weeds around the New England asters in the north garden, and I walked Bella through the alley to the whistling of starlings and the calls of cardinals. Around noon, there was a brief shower, and then in the afternoon, the temperature climbed high into the middle 60s, the sky became hazy, and the low sun shone through altostratus clouds, white in the southwest.

Last night, I had been reading predictions about the end of the world (on the occasion of the alignment of this December's solstice with the Galactic equator, a once-in-twenty-six-thousand-years event, foretold by the ancient

Mayas). All that foolishness, along with the longest nights of the year, had somehow set me off balance, and I decided to go and see for myself what was happening to the world of South Glen.

I walked along the river, the water higher than it had been in months. Robins were clucking down the path where blackberry branches had new leaves. Garlic mustard that had escaped the mustard pullers was growing up defiantly beside Osage fruits shredded by squirrels. Henbit and sweet rockets and wild onions, ragwort and feathery hemlock and floppy leafcup pushed out between the mossy trunks of fallen trees. In the muck beyond the covered bridge, skunk cabbage was set for March. And all around me soft, green mounds of mouse-eared chickweed were rising through layers of the last honeysuckle leaves, through the crumbling strata of summer and fall, along the bottom land and up the wooded talus slopes.

My favorite companion on December walks, the mouse-eared chickweed sprouts in late August or September, and grows steadily through the darkest seasons into spring. Untroubled by heavy snow or deep cold, it takes advantage of intermittent thaws to grow across the forest floor. Sometimes, chickweed buds by the end of January. Even in average years, it is one of the earliest of flowering plants, its blossoms holding from February through April.

Encouraged by this year's gentle autumn, the mouse-eared chickweed rose tightly and firmly around the other precocious weeds, binding and linking them, leading them in forecast for a new year. Glowing in the late sun, their small, bold leaves seemed to me a bright banner of hope spreading through the Glen, and a fresh antidote to apocalypse.

Indeed, I saw, there truly was a great convergence in the making, albeit not the one the Mayas had in mind. For the rising mouse-eared chickweed, the garlic mustard, the ragwort, the sweet rocket, the henbit, the moss, the skunk cabbage, the hemlock and the wild onions were aligned as plainly as any galactic objects could ever be, earthstars shining day and night across the winter to come.

2014: Two large murmurations of starlings seen on the way to

Cincinnati today. And Casey called at 12:23 this afternoon: "There's a gigantic murder of crows up at the county line at Polecat Road," he said. "Hundreds and hundreds of them. The wind's blowing and they're just jumping up and down and floating around. Must be something up there that brings them in because I've seen them there other years. But there are lots and lots of them today, enjoying the sun and the breeze."

2016: Leaves on the euonymus vine on the north side of the house are becoming a creamy gold, the color of the berries' outer hulls, and have started to fall. A few starlings chattering in a bare silver maple along Limestone Street after sunrise.

2017: A fat camel cricket in the bathtub this morning, perhaps emboldened by tonight's "Supermoon." Mild and clear weather persists. A few more robins seen.

2018: After yesterday's warmth and hard wind, Early Winter arrived today with clouds and cold and icy mist. Most of the Osage fruits along the street have turned splotchy brown.

2020: John Blakelock called to report that his friend Doug had seen sandhill cranes flying over his farm just north of Spring Valley today and yesterday.

When you give yourself to places, they give you yourself back; the more one comes to know them, the more one seeds them with the invisible crop of memories and associations that will be waiting for you when you come back, while new places offer up new thoughts, new possibilities.

Rebecca Solnit

December 4th
The 338th Day of the Year

Through his iron glades
Rides Winter the Huntsman.
All color fades
As his horn is heard sighing.

Osbert Sitwell

Sunrise/set: 7:40/5:10
Day's Length: 9 hours 30 minutes
Average High/Low: 43/28
Average Temperature: 35
Record High: 66 – 1982, 67 – 2001
Record Low: 9 – 1935

The Daily Weather

Highs remain in the teens or 20s five percent of the days, are in the 30s six years in ten, warm into the 40s twenty percent of the time, into the 50 ten percent, and into the 60s five percent. Rain or snow falls one year in three. Clouds are more common than sun; overcast conditions occur 55 percent of the time.

The Natural Calendar

The old Yellow Springs year of sprouting, growing and producing fruit has fallen away with the leaves and the end of harvest, and the first week of Early Winter marks the beginning of a new cycle in Earth's spin around the sun.

Seasons are local, fluid constructs that take their own direction from both meteorological as well as geographical cues. Our winter no more actually starts at December solstice than summer starts at June solstice. The "natural year" recognizes that process and gives it a shape closer to what actually occurs around us.

Even though pear trees sometimes hold out and a few honeysuckles and some privets keep their foliage, the buds of next spring are already showing, and the skunk cabbage of February and pussy willow catkins of March are poised to expand in each thaw to

29

come.

Now the asters, milkweed and boneset, virgin's bower, winterberry, honeysuckle and bittersweet set their seeds more quickly. Gauges of passage appear across the ground, the Osage fruits decaying, sometimes opened and scattered by squirrels, the hulls of black walnuts pocked and stained, heaps of leaves darkening, settling, contracting, dissolving.

On the early cusp of winter, Lenten roses gradually show their buds as crocus and snowdrops pierce the soft mulch and hold immune to cold beneath the snow. Sap quivers in the maples every thaw. Migrations overlap, the last sandhill cranes high over the first new bluebirds. The long nights urge the foxes to mate. Owls lay out their nests.

In all of this there is a correspondence with the new year's movement throughout the country. Gauges of a local season are always gauges of a distant season. Knowing home, a watcher measures faraway time. A parochial thermometer not only displays alternating waves of mild or bitter weather but also counts out the days of the finite winter road that begins in the snow and ends on the warm beaches of the South. There the camellia, bougainvillea, flame vine, Hong Kong orchid tree, jasmine, and powderpuff bloom. Oranges, grapefruit, papayas, carambola and avocados ripen for picking.

Daybook

1982: Unusual early December warm spell, new record high of 66 today. Purple deadnettle, catnip, chickweed, henbit continue to grow as if it were spring.

1983: Sparrows chirping steadily much of the morning and afternoon. One dandelion blooming in the melting snow. One robin in the back hedge.

1984: Red-tailed hawk seen on the way to Wilberforce. In town, a few beech leaves still hold along Dayton Street, a third of the forsythia too. After last night's hard freeze, silver maples are withering. The pears downtown thin quickly.

1986: The decadence of Late Fall stops now. The landscape is complete for the next three months. The fishing hole, Middle Prairie, and Far Prairie will remain quiet and stable, bare and predictable.

1988: The greenhouse so quiet this morning. The sun is just beginning to show against the west wall on the highest leaves of the biggest poinsettia. Robin seen in the yard today. Was it the same one I saw last week; is it wintering over in the honeysuckles?

1989: Winter colors forming all around me, blacks, browns, grays, with red berries and patches of green and yellow green along the paths.

1992: The pear foliage on Xenia Avenue holds at maybe a tenth of their leaves. Geese fly over at 12:35 p.m. South Glen this afternoon, cloudy, 40 degrees, light wind: Clover foliage keeping the paths green, with some dandelions, some plantain. Wind in the dry grass, oak leaves rustling, distant crows intermittent, no other birds for the first miles. Then the scream of a robin as though he were frightened or had been attacked.

Craneflies follow me up into High Prairie. Moss is still bright beside me, becomes the dominant green in the woods. A few red raspberry leaves at the top of the hill, an occasional bank of honeysuckle berries. Nettles, protected by wild roses, grow back in the valley, a foot tall. Top sweet gum seed balls hold. Teasel dark in the dull goldenrod fields.

Osage all yellow on the ground. Pale greens and pastels of the lichens. Then the landscape down the valley: bands of grays and browns above a sky of light stratus clouds. The trees black, pasture chartreuse: a cross section of the winter, veins of this time. On the footbridge from Jacoby, walnut hulls, shredded, staining the wood purple. Coming back, I saw a pair of flickers; they screeched then flew west off toward the river. At Sycamore Hole, three tan moths, between half an inch and an inch wingspan, struggled through the cold. I fished there: only one bite.

Today, the listing of the pieces of the last season is complete, and they become fragments of a new season, Early Winter, the first season of the New Year.

1993: Flowers of the caraway – which volunteered from seed when the ferns were planted last May – have finally turned brown.

1997: Bradford pear leaves are yellow and black, maybe three-fourths down. Neysa says the sparrows still chant in the trees outside her Xenia Avenue apartment half an hour before dawn.

2002: Leaves withered on the spirea and butterfly bush from cold in the teens this morning. The pond has started to freeze over.

2005: Medium-sized camel cricket found floating in the dog's water this morning.

2006: From Yellow Springs south to Asheville, NC. Sun and cold throughout the day. The roadside grass definitely grew greener as we drove down I-75. Some honeysuckle leaves were left on bushes near Lexington and then again at Knoxville, but no other foliage observed except on one white oak. Flocks of starlings seen off and on throughout, one flock feasting on honeysuckle berries. The full moon came up at 5:15 as the sun went down behind us.

2007: At five to eleven yesterday, Casey called on his cell. He was taking the back way to Springfield, north down Polecat Road, when he saw all the crows. "It's a murder of crows!" he said, and I could hear the excitement in his voice. "They're all over in the fields on either side of the road just past Ellis Pond."

I took Bella, the family dog, jumped into the truck and headed out to watch what was going on. I could see crows all the way from Fairfield Pike, and I drove slowly down the hill into the feeding murder (a murder being the correct name for a crow flock – and not some senseless slaughter).

Bella was as fascinated as I was as we moved through the birds at maybe ten miles and hour. They were cleaning up the soybean field on the east side of Polecat and the cornfield on the west side. I had counted about a hundred starlings in Mateo's black walnut tree earlier that morning, and I could tell there were hundreds of crows, maybe a thousand, around us. They were indifferent to traffic, and they crossed the road leisurely, floating up to let the cars go by and settling down to feed. Tame as hungry gulls at the beach or honeybees around their hive, the crows were masters of the landscape.

I thought they might stay and spend the winter near the pond (like they sometimes do a little further north of town), but they were gone the next day. Still, there was more news. Casey called again. This time he was unloading a pickup near the Antioch golf course and saw sandhill cranes flying over Glen Helen, the first flock around 11:30 in the morning, making "that long whistling sound, almost a yodel." He went home for lunch and heard another flock "coming right over the house. Wilma saw them, too!" They were heading south, of course, flying hard, Casey said, "in front of that storm coming in from the northwest."

2009: The gooseneck loosestrife foliage is browning now, losing its autumn reds and golds. In the alley, the thin-leafed coneflower was shriveled from last night's frost. Jeanie reported eight buzzards in the roost along Corey Street this morning. The rest of the Osage leaves came down today, the last covering of golden foliage on the lawn by the shed. I think about my assertion the other day that the natural year starts with the beginning of December. I feel that something has turned now, that there is nothing left to hold on to, that some kind of dam has broken, and that the cold is the rush of cleansing and scrubbing and renewing.

2010: The two flowering cabbages I planted yesterday are covered with snow today.

2011: The hobblebush has lost most of its pale yellow leaves this past week, darkening the back yard.

2012: Another gentle day in the 60s: I walked Bella at 8:45 this morning, encountered a great flock of starlings, accompanied by several crows and by the sounds also of robins settling into the cottonwoods along Dayton Street and the high maples along Limestone.

2014: Last night, a vole drowned (under the waxing Marauding Mouse Moon) in the dog's water dish! Now the December 3rd cold front settles in. Crows near 8:00 this morning. Light flurries, a few murmurations of starlings, through the day.

33

2016: Clouds, quiet, 35 degrees: Once again, a walk after sunrise down Limestone Street: robins peeping, starlings chattering and whistling, crows in the distance.

2017: A mild afternoon, cloudy, balanced on 60 degrees, rain due. I took the leaf netting from the pond, and the fish slowly, almost indifferently rose to eat the handful of food I gave them.

2019: Sunny and mild today. On the pond, the water was deep blue, speckled with a hundred black and white geese, shining.

2020: Jenny Cowperthwaite Ruka and Liz Porter both sent me videos of sandhill cranes flying over John Bryan Park around 3:00 this afternoon. "They were flying toward the SW and then looped in circles around the river for a little while before they flew on," wrote Liz. "It's been years for me since I've seen them, and it was a thrill."

The moon will be your Grandmother. And she will have special duties. She will give moisture to dampen the land at night. She will also move the tides. Along with the moon there will be stars. The stars help give us directions when we travel and, along with Grandmother Moon, tell us when we should begin our ceremonies.

Onondaga Chief Powless

December 5th
The 339th Day of the Year

I rejoice in the winter landscape, cut to essentials.
Earth and sky are more closely joined.

Harlan Hubbard

Sunrise/set: 7:41/5:10
Day's Length: 9 hours 29 minutes
Average High/Low: 42/27
Average Temperature: 35
Record High: 67 – 1998
Record Low: 6 – 1901

The Daily Weather
Today's high temperature distribution is as follows: 20 percent chance of 50s, forty percent for 40s, thirty percent for 30s, and 10 percent for 20s or teens. Skies are overcast half the time; chances of precipitation: 35 percent. Until 1994, December 5th was the latest date for snow in central Ohio. The record was broken that December, the latest date moved to December 10th.

The Natural Calendar
Before the arrival of deep cold, snapdragons and yarrow can still be budding. The dead nettle, *Lamium purpureum,* still has blossoms. Basal leaf clusters grow back on carnations, dock, sweet rockets, chickweed, purple deadnettle, celandine, garlic mustard, poppies, lamb's ear and daisies. Until the hardest frost, St. John's wort, lavender, butterfly bush, euonymus and Japanese honeysuckle keep their leaves. The mint is still fragrant. Parsley and thyme can still be green and firm for seasoning.

The Sun
The sun reaches a declination of 22 degrees, 22 minutes on the 5th of December, approximately one degree from its declination at winter solstice. The sun's position will remain within a degree of solstice until January 8th, producing a period of solar stability similar

to the one between June 4th and July 8th.

Daybook

1984: Forsythia leaves give way to the hard freezes. Beets and Chinese cabbage survive five days of very cold temperatures. First greenhouse tomatoes, planted on July 16th, harvested today.

1989: Cardinal sings sporadically through the day.

1994: Cress is reaching up from the water now. Garlic mustard continues to grow taller. The first and second cold fronts of December have failed to arrive (there have only been five mornings of frost since May), and Second Spring keeps coming. Cardinals singing off and on through the morning.

1997: Crows and blue jays this morning at 8:08 a.m. I worked in the garden in the middle of flurries, turning over the ground, changing the snow into black, wet soil. Overcast most of the day and humid, the sun showing up just a few minutes about four o'clock. The pond temperature is down to 42 degrees, and the fish huddle motionless at the bottom near the water pump. It felt like the first day of Early Winter today.

1998: New record high of 67 today.

2000: Camel cricket killed in the house by one of the cats last night.

2001: Shirt-sleeve day. Cardinals sang early, then off and on through the morning. In the campus lawn: dandelions, shepherd's purse, clover, and sow thistles were blooming. The afternoon was calm and soft and sweet, sky hazy blue, light breeze, the grass brightening after an initial November yellowing. Treetops bare and lean. Forsythia in full bloom on Winter Street. Even one of our bushes along the east fence has flowered.

2006: Asheville, North Carolina to Daytona Beach, Florida. In Asheville, the air was cool, not a cloud in the sky, temperatures in the 50s. Coming out of the mountains this morning, about 100 miles northwest of Columbia, South Carolina, we began to see some foliage on white oaks and red oaks. Below Columbia, the foliage grew thicker, much thicker by Savannah and Brunswick. Sweet gums and yellow poplars joined the growing sense of autumn's return. Below Jacksonville, the habitat changed again, the color of the waysides almost solid green. Two myrtle flowers bloomed at a rest stop near St. Augustine. Back home in Yellow Springs, a tremendous high-pressure system is bringing temperatures into the teens again tonight.

2007: First snow of the season last night and this morning, four to five inches. The sparrows are ravenous at the feeder, but the rest of High Street is quiet, no starlings in Don's tree, no starling chatter in the neighborhood. The alley bamboo is full of snow, bowing and blocking the east side of my path there. At home, our bamboo has arched over the half-frozen pond. Large camel cricket found on the bedroom floor.

2008: Temperature in the teens this morning, light flurries, sun trying to come through. Only one bird chirp heard as I walked the alley. Downtown, the pears are thinning, but along Elm Street, the younger pears are still full. The beech tree on Dayton Street has kept much of its foliage, but the leaves are twisted and shriveled from the cold. Two flocks of starlings seen on the way to Beavercreek.

2009: Along High Street, one periwinkle flower, legacy of the mild November, soft blue against the frost.

2010: Two inches of snow yesterday, and the temperature is not supposed to rise above freezing for several days. Crows at 7:40 this morning. Casey called and left a message while we were out shopping: "The sandhill cranes are moving over up above the snow. Here they come, moving to the southeast, definitely the sandhill cranes, probably 40 or 50 of them cruising along just at the top of the snow."

    And a note from Liz: "I just tried to call you, but your line was busy. About 2:00 p.m. I stepped out my back door, and lo and behold! The best gift I could ask for: sandhill cranes flying and clucking/purring their way south approximately above Mills Lawn/Xenia Avenue area. I hope you got to see them, or others. They carry magic." Then Ed Oxley's report: five buzzards eating a deer carcass. He thought it was kind of strange that they were here so late in the year.

2011: Crows at 7:26 this morning, rain and mild. The rain increased through the day as the wind switched to the northwest, all the brooks and rivers very high, great pools of water in the fields and in the yard.

2012: To the Indian Mound near Cedarville with Jeff: River high from the last two days of rain. Many white mushrooms with brownish tops eaten off by deer or other creatures found along the path. The fungi appear to be *Callybia butyracea.*

2014: At Peggy's, dock and lamb's ear growing back. At home, henbit, bittercress and chickweed that sprouted in the fall are starting to spread a little as the cold fronts arrive then soften quickly. Along High Street, the outer layer of Osage fruits has darkened, spotted with age.

2016: The pears and the Dayton Street beech tree keep only patches of leaves.

2019: At 7:10 this clear, chilly morning, long cardinal songs, then a robin whinny, then crows calling, then quiet.

There can never be enough scientists or humanists to gather the simple, quotidian facts of every existing thing, even though accurately understanding the world demands no less.

William Least Heat-Moon

December 6th
The 340th Day of the Year

If we are to live in the present, being truly alive, then everything recedes except these simple things that we observe, these particular movements that we make, a walk in the garden, the watching of birds.

Robert Orwell, O.S.B.

Sunrise/set: 7:42/5:10
Day's Length: 9 hours 28 minutes
Average High/Low: 42/27
Average Temperature: 35
Record High: 70 – 1956
Record Low: - 1 – 1977

The Daily Weather
There is a five percent chance of highs in the 60s or 70s, twenty percent for 50s, thirty-five for 40s, twenty percent for 30s, fifteen percent for 20s, and five percent for teens. Chances of rain today are 35 percent, for snow 15 percent, and totally overcast conditions occur six years in a decade. This is the last day for a slight chance of a high above 70 until January 21st in most areas of the Lower Midwest and Middle Atlantic region. And from today until March 1st, record low temperatures remain below zero.

The Natural Calendar
The second major cold front of December often ushers in Early Winter between the 8th and the 10th. This three-week season usually puts an end to the milder weather of late autumn, creating a bridge to the harsher conditions of Deep Winter that develop by January 1.
Early Winter closes the Season of Second Spring, the Season of Late Autumn Crocus Bloom, the Poinsettia Shipment Season, the Season of Bittersweet Shedding, the Corn and Soybean Harvest Season. Leafdrop Season is almost complete for almost every tree. In the garden, Strawberry Mulching Season complements Herb Transplanting Season, the time to transfer oregano, rosemary,

parsley, thyme and sage to indoor pots. Fertilizing Season for field and garden continues through next month.

Daybook

1986: South Glen, 37 degrees: One duck on the river, two kingfishers chasing back and forth, sparrows chattering, milkweed pods half open, disheveled seeds half out in the wind, Osage fruits yellowing, broken and scattered by squirrels or opossums, parsnips burned from frost, goldenrod and asters in tufts, heads of the iron week still intact, pale and soft, craneflies swarming, honeysuckle berries and red rose hips holding (and two new rose leaves pushing out), oak bark black and shining, white sycamores, purple raspberry stalks, gray-blue clouds, woodpeckers rattling on the far side of the field. At Jacoby swamp, skunk cabbage is six inches high. The river was up almost two feet, the opposite of last year. No trace of the long patches of lizard's tail that bloomed along the banks in July.

1987: Covered Bridge: Skunk cabbage up, all of Second Spring's growth steady. Flock of ducks on the river. Some new wild rose leaves have sprouted.

1988: Paperwhites, which started growing on November 22nd, are in full bloom now. Amaryllis, watered on the 13th, is just beginning to open. All the Christmas cacti are in full bloom. Greenhouse tomatoes are coming in steadily. Knuckles of rhubarb are up in the garden, kale continuing to grow in the warmest fall I remember. Second Spring everywhere in the woods. A cardinal sang at 10:00 a.m.

1989: Geese fly over the house, honking at 11:58 a.m., also at about 3:00, again at sundown.

1991: I was measuring things this afternoon, and came to the leaf pile. I had waded through it at the end of October, all the leaves from the yard up to my waist; they've settled a little since then, a foot or so in just a month; by spring, they'll be flat and dense, full of night crawlers, ready to dig under.

1997: To Canton in northern Ohio and back today. Snow blowing hard, it was a real winter day, gusty and bitter, temperatures in the

20s, sky slate gray, only a minute or so in the afternoon when the sun was visible. The snow was heavy and wet, sticking to the ground as we went walking around in Zoar. The floors of the stores and houses we visited had puddles and stains from everyone's boots. As we went down one street, Jeni found a worm lying out on the ground; it was dead, but we couldn't decide how or why it had been out on such a cold day.

1998: The last Osage leaves came down today; I'll have to rake one more time in the back yard.

1999: By the wood stove in the greenhouse, the Christmas cacti are all coming in, the pale pink ones completely open, the darker colors not far behind. All the geraniums are blooming, tomatoes ripening.

2002: Pond half frozen in this bitter Early Winter. Sweet Cicely seedpods are sharp black crescents. Thistles are bedraggled and sagging. Angelica is hollow and broken. Wingstem is leaning, its leaves twisted, tight around its stalks. Asters and ironweed tufts are coming undone. River still open, some ice in the sloughs.

2005: Deep freeze settling over the region. The pond is three-fourths frozen over. The starlings no longer cackle in the trees along the alley. No robins seen. The oakleaf hydrangea leaves have curled and blackened in the cold, lows in the single digits. Camel cricket found in the laundry room this evening.

2006: Daytona Beach to Miami Beach, Florida. A new cold wave has moved down across the Midwest deep into the South, Jekyll Island in Georgia having a high of only 46 on Friday. The drive to Miami revealed more of the retreat from autumn, more green deciduous trees, sweet gums, maples, oaks, fewer clumps of mistletoe visible in bare branches, summer and the tropics reasserting themselves from the Caribbean, blending with the end of the old year, foretelling the changes that will reach Georgia in February. Here in Miami Beach, weeds and shrubs are in flower, but less exuberantly than I saw on our trip to Key West last year. The egrets we usually see at Jekyll in the early spring are now in central and southern Florida.

2008: Cold wind from the southwest, flurries, temperatures only in the teens: Early Winter is here. The pond is frozen over except for where the thin waterfall enters the water. No birds seen or heard on the alley walk this morning, no finches at the finch bags, but chickadees and sparrows at the feeders. Leaves on the ground continue to turn to a uniform dull brown. In the greenhouse, the Christmas cacti continue in bloom, as do the paperwhites we started the first week of November. The amaryllis, though, has just pushed up about an inch, even after three weeks.

2009: The morning bright with sun and frost, silence in the alley, ice on the pond all the way to the waterfall, all the November plants prostrate from the cold. In the north garden, the rose leaves hold deep green. Along the east hedge, the Japanese honeysuckle keeps a border with the street. Jeanie watched the sparrows trying to drink from the pond, tapping the ice with their beaks, coming back, doing it again in disbelief.

2010: Crows at 7:43 a.m. Deep cold pushes down from Canada, bringing a freeze to central Florida tonight and tomorrow night. In the Northeast and along the Great Lakes, up to two feet of lake-effect snow so far this month. The pond in the back yard is frozen over except at the waterfall.

2015: Riding in bright sun with Jill late afternoon across central Ohio: all the pastures and wheat fields bright green after a November six degrees above average and a mild start to December. At the state park north of Columbus, frost lay across the drifts of goldenrod. One rose had budded in Delaware, Ohio. Two murmurations of starlings seen in plowed fields along the highway. From Vermont, Cathy writes that there is still no snow on the ground there, highs in the 40s. In the pond at home, the koi are sluggish but still interested in food.

2016: Cold and rainy, Zelcovas and the beech down to just their bottom leaves.

2017: Deep cold, this morning pulled across Ohio by the full moon at perigee.

Ed Oxley called about nine o'clock, saying that when the

river flooded his property a few weeks ago, the water had washed away the leaves and revealed snowdrops an inch tall. And blackbirds, he said, hundreds of them, were feeding on honeysuckle berries, intermittently swooping down to eat and then swooping back up to the trees. Then Rick wrote: "I was out in John Bryan when a whirlwind of cedar waxwings came roaring through. Ain't never seen so many, like leaves on the trees. At first thought they were blackbirds, they were making so much noise."

I suppose his observations and mine are far more personal scaffolding rather than natural history. I read the other day about a 90-year-old woman in Japan who had kept a record of each day in her housing complex since her husband and daughter died forty year previously. She said it was comforting to make that daily structure, even though no one would read it and that it would probably be thrown away when she died. So with my scaffolding of flowers and birds and insects and weather.... What can I expect? The body of notes is like the physical human body. One can take apart the body and find only flesh and blood and bone. Daybooks under the knife reveal only pages and letters of the alphabet. Life and soul and connection and coherence lie elsewhere.

2019: A cardinal dialogue this morning at 7:20, then silence. The day is cloudy and mild, a calm before the precipitation and then the cold to come. The sand hill cranes knew about the weather to come: At 11:50. Betty called to say she had seen a tremendous "V" of more than a hundred of them right over High and Whiteman Streets, just a little way from my house. I was working inside and, of course, didn't hear them. Then Jon Whitmore called at 12:30 to say he had also seen "about forty" cranes less than a mile west of town.

Ah, soon on field and hill
The wind shall whistle chill.

George Arnold

December 7th
The 341st Day of the Year

You can see things better in the winter. You can see the shapes of the trees better, like how the oaks are different from the maples. And the form of the garden here, the way the snow will melt on the ground, but stay white on the path and bricks.

Frances Hurie, 20th Century Yellow Springs Teacher

Sunrise/set: 7:43/5:10
Day's Length: 9 hours 27 minutes
Average High/Low: 42/27
Average Temperature: 34
Record High: 67 – 1892
Record Low: - 1 – 1977

The Daily Weather

Today's high temperatures are in the 50s thirty percent of the years, in the 40s another 30 percent, in the 30s twenty-five percent, 15 percent in the 20s or teens. The sky is completely overcast 45 percent of the time, and chances of rain are 30 percent, for snow five to ten percent. The 16-week snow period begins for Ohio within the next seven days, with frozen precipitation up to four inches recorded in the Dayton area seven years in ten within the next week.

The Natural Calendar

The normal seasons need no predictions. The averages around which we plan our lives are fixed by history, and they hold true seven or eight out of every ten years.

December nights are usually in the middle and upper 20s throughout Ohio, and typical highs reach about 45 in southern counties and those along Lake Erie, only 35 in the mountains and the central counties. January is the most extreme of the three winter months, highs averaging only in the 30s, and nighttime temperatures usually in the teens and 20s. February is typically about like December.

The dates for deepest cold are readily available to anyone who keeps a weather journal. In general, the third week of

December, the first 20 days of January and the first seven days of February are the most frigid of the year. If it's going to be a terrible winter, the worst winds will blow during these five weeks.

From another perspective, just ten fronts out of the winter's 20 are usually severe. The approximate days (predicable within 48 hours either way) for the arrival of those air systems are December 8, 15, 20, January 1, 5, 11, 15, February 2, 7, 12.

Snow usually accompanies most of these fronts. In the northern part of the state, normal snowfall for December, January and February totals about 25 inches. Central counties: 17 inches. Southern counties: 10 inches.

But is there a chance for a bitter cold and stormy winter like the one that hit back in '78? The odds are always against it. Great freezes are rare. The past century has only produced a dozen bone- chilling Decembers, the most recent to the end of the 20th century occurring in 1983 when five dawns registered below zero, and temperatures stayed below 20 for a full seven days. January is always the most dramatic month for cold. But only 14 of the last 100 have been exceptionally fierce. And just ten Februarys have been unusually cool since the end of the 19th century.

And what are the odds for all three months being completely   cold? About three in 100: the closest the area ever came to such a winter was in 1884 -1885, 1962 - 1963 and 1977-1978.

Daybook

1984: After five days of winter, fierce temperatures, six inches of snow, the pear leaves still hold on, brown and leathery. Beech and forsythia leaves continue in patches.

1985: Broccoli, horseradish and rhubarb killed off by several days of weather in the teens. Deep green parsley and dusky-leafed thyme still alive under their mulch. All the leaves finally came down from Becky's white birch.

1986: Cardinal sings 8:31 a.m. then silent. Sparrow hawk seen along

Grinnell Road.

1987: Sparrows loud in the bare forsythia off and on through the day.

1992: Cardinal sings at 8:20 a.m. in the snow. Sage still fully green and fragrant downtown.

1997: A gentle, damp winter day, maybe two inches of snow on the ground from yesterday's storm. The temperature was in the middle 30s this afternoon. As I walked, I could open my coat, even though my feet got cold in the wet mud and grass. The wind was down, and the sky rolled slowly by in broad bands of pastel grays, some lighter, some darker. The snow was soft, good for snowballs or snowmen, but there was barely enough on the ground for either. Melting was spotty, leaving the ground dappled in white and brown. I wanted to name all the browns I saw, from the pale champagnes of the field grass, goldenrod and ironweed seed tufts, to the russets of the leaves of Japanese knotweed hanging to their stems, to the deep dark browns of the tree barks. And all were reflected in the river so quiet that it took each object and color without distortion, snow and chocolate and charcoal branches and the alternate bright and dull waves of sky.

1998: The warmest fall I remember ended today. Highs were only in the 40s, Early Winter approaching on schedule.

1999: Strei updates me from Fort Lauderdale: "I'm about ready to plant a vegetable garden on the flat roof part of my house because that's where there's most sun. My herb garden is now planted -- basil, oregano, nasturtiums, parsley – all are doing well. After [SEP]Hurricane Irene busted a number of my corn plants (dracaenas), I've managed to restart them as pups and they are now ready to be given as plant gifts for Christmas. This particular dracaena is about to bloom and gives off a wonderful scent in the evening and night hours. The mangos are in full bloom now and will produce fruit for harvest in late June through August. My grapefruits have really put out this year. My red ruby seedless variety tree has about 150 grapefruit on it, and they'll be ready to eat next week and through February. My navel oranges are doing so-so, only about 50 on the tree."

2000: Camel cricket in the hallway, 8:45 p.m.

2003: Starlings still cackling in the village trees. The downtown pears and the Dayton Street beech still hold on to a few leaves.

2004: The small-flowered hollyhock continues to bloom in the mild days. Some green leaves remain on the butterfly bush. In the garden, the chard is still quite strong, but the broccoli plants I set out in August only have heads an inch or so across.

2007: More snow this morning, about five inches on the ground now. Brown, stiff Osage leaves spiral down and stick up in the snow. The new bird feeder by the bedroom window has attracted a purple finch, a female cardinal, and a chickadee. The sparrows are still at the front feeder. Oakleaf hydrangea leaves are darkening and curling from the cold. The pond is more than half frozen over. In the greenhouse, the Christmas cacti have pretty much completed their blooming, and all the tomatoes planted in July are ripe, the plants way past their best.

2008: Crows flew over yard, high in the cold at 7:40 this morning. Light snow on the ground, hazy sky. No birdsong through the first part of the day. Then Casey called at 1:57 p.m.: "Get outside quick," he said. "There's around fifty sandhill cranes flying over, they're right about at the college…."

　　　I ran out, couldn't see them, but heard them calling in the distance.

2009: First light snow of the year this morning. Privet bushes along Limestone are almost bare now, and the honeysuckle berries have almost disappeared.

2010: At 4:45 this afternoon, Casey called from Nash Road, about ten miles east of Yellow Springs. "I saw about a dozen sandhill cranes flying high and southeast," he said, "but they weren't making a sound, just winging along with the northwest wind."

 2012: A large flock of starlings settled around the west end of town this morning, stayed for hours, whistling and clucking. Occasional robins still heard off and on.

2013: Ruth Page sighted sandhills at 4:17 in the afternoon above the corner of Corry and Xenia Avenue. "I heard the sound and looked up," said Ruth, "and there they were."

2016: The cold gathers strength, more cold on the way, the Osage leaves trickle to the ground. Maybe tomorrow or the next day they'll be all down.

2017: Driving north to Springfield, I passed a large murder of crows near Whitehall Farm. Like last year, more deep cold moving in, snow maybe tomorrow, and the Osage leaves trickle down, the last leaves of the beech and Zelcovas and Lil's maple seem frozen in place. Last night brought a thin layer of ice to most of the pond, ice for the first time since last winter. This morning on the way to the shed, I saw the first snowflakes of the year.

2018: At 1:15 in the afternoon, the sky was clear. One contrail far in the north followed a tiny shining jet. The temperature was just at freezing, barometer very high at 30.50, light wind from the west-southwest

I was coming back from walking with Ranger, my border collie, when I heard what sounded like pigeons calling. Or was it owls? Of course, the sound could have been neither pigeons nor owls. Yellow Springs has no pigeons, and all the owls were sleeping.

I looked and looked, but saw nothing. Then I wondered: Could it be sandhill cranes? Was my hearing loss allowing me to only hear the lower tones of their cries?

When I got home around 1:30, Anne called: She had been watching two flocks of sandhill cranes "almost right over our neighborhood, Birch III at the south end of town. The first flock of about 30 cranes was kind of hovering around, and then they kind of mingled with the second flock, which was about 30 cranes, too. Then the first flock went off toward the south, and the second still hovered so high I could barely see them, almost mingling with a cloud...."⸢┐⸣SEP

A few minutes later, Aida called: "I'm walking on Hyde and Corry," she said, "and they are flying high over my

49

head. They got my attention because they were making a racket. O my gosh – about 40 cranes… they are very high up! I read about them last week in the paper, but here I am enjoying them all over again."

2019: Yesterday's crane sightings preceded this mornings abrupt rise in the barometer. Robins peeping in the yard as I stacked wood.

2020: Ed Oxley reports a honeybee.

Journal: Mice in the Mug

Wee, sleeket, cowran, tim'rous beastie,
O, what panic's in thy breastie!
Thou need na start awa sae hasty,
Wi' bickering brattle!
I wad be laith to rin an' chase thee,
Wi' murd'ring pattle!

Robert Burns

I keep my birdseed in plastic container inside a small shed behind the house, and the other morning I forgot to put the cover back on the container.

When I went out to feed the birds the following day, I discovered at the bottom of the near-empty container, a mouse peering out from the coffee mug I used to scoop the seed. Its nose was quivering like a dog's (at least I remember it that way), and its eyes were huge and black. It had fallen into the container, hulled numerous sunflower seeds, but then had been unable to climb out.

So I took the container outside to dump the cup and mouse, and feed the birds. But when I looked down once more, a second mouse appeared from out of the cup and then a third: three fat, frightened mice packed into a coffee mug, coming out to look at me and then retreating back into the highly inadequate shelter, stuffing themselves so tightly that only their tails stuck out.

I stood in the snow, imagining their panic and their dread. Certainly, they might have known I was their adversary. I had killed so many of their kind in traps winter after winter when they had invaded my porous house to find warmth and crumbs. They had little reason to hope for clemency.

But the more I thought about what they might be feeling, the more I became entangled with myself. Shamelessly I anthropomorphized those mice, projecting my own fears and regrets upon them. Suddenly their predicament stood for all the foolish, reckless, thoughtless, ill-advised things I had ever done in my life, things so stupid that I try to forget them all the time but never quite succeed.

I made a general confession of my failures to the mice, telling them things I had hidden for so long, admitting to them things I could not have told a human soul. And it felt so good, talking to these compatriots in crime, that, for just a moment, it seemed a fearsome burden had been lifted from me and that my transgressions had been absolved.

Slowly I reached down and lifted the cup, spilled its contents close to a space under the shed where the mice could escape. They stood for an instant in the snow, their pelts shining, priestly dark, their fat black eyes searching mine, and then they scurried for safety.

"Go, and sin no more," I told them (and myself), placing a little extra seed around the hole into which they disappeared.

For a few days, they were on their best behavior. I decided that they must have understood all I told them, that they had learned from their mistakes and mine, and that they had realized, as Robert Burns wrote, how "the best laid schemes o' Mice an' Men,/Gang aft agley,/An' lea'e us nought but grief an' pain,/ For promis'd joy!"

Then yesterday, I found a small hole gnawed into the side of the seed container near the tightly fastened lid. This time, there were four mice in the mug.

Heap on more wood! The wind is chill,
But let it whistle as it will,
We'll keep our Christmas merry still.

Sir Walter Scott

51

Thou best of men and friends! We will create
A genuine summer in each other's breast,
And spite of this cold time and frozen fate,
Thaw us a warm seat to our rest.

Richard Lovelace

Sunrise/set: 7:44/5:10
Day's Length: 9 hours 26 minutes
Average High/Low: 41/26
Average Temperature: 33
Record High: 68 – 1883
Record Low: - 3 – 1917

The Daily Weather

Early Winter normally usually begins in the Lower Midwest no later than this date, with the first of the season's 16 major cold fronts. By today, the possibility of snow is now 30 percent greater than it was at the end of November, and frozen precipitation falls more frequently today and on the 10th, than on any other days in the first two weeks of December. Today's typical temperature distribution: five percent of the highs are in the 60s, five percent in the 50s, thirty percent in the 40s, forty percent in the 30s, twenty percent in the 20s. The shines on four to five days out of ten. Rain comes ten percent of the days, snow on 20 percent. Freezing nighttime temperatures occur 85 percent of the nights.

The Weather in the Week Ahead

This week of the year typically brings the second major cold front of the month between the 8th and the 10th, and the third high-pressure system between the 11th and the 13th. Completely overcast skies dominate 60 percent of the days, and precipitation often occurs as the cold waves approach. Afternoon highs are usually in the 20s or 30s (a 55 percent chance of temperatures so cold). The 10th and the 12th are the days this week with the best chance of warmth in the 50s (slightly better than a 30 percent chance of that), and severe weather with below-zero temperatures and highs only in the teens is rare.

The Natural Calendar

Almost every leaf has fallen by this time of December; even the most stubborn Osage, pear and beech are down. Trunks of the rusty-barked river birches and the white birches contrast with the red-twigged dogwoods, and with the black trunks of oaks and elms.

Daybook

1982: Flocks of sparrows were working the goldenrod seeds at South Glen this afternoon.

1983: Two flocks of doves seen on Grinnell today.

1986: Giant murder of crows, hundreds of them, in the soybean fields along the highway east of Springfield.

1989: First junco seen at the bird feeder.

1993: South Glen: Flock of more than a dozen robins feeding on the green path to the Butterfly Preserve. Flying with them, a band of flickers. A great blue heron flew over along the river, the third seen so far this month.

1994: Upstream toward the Covered Bridge about four this afternoon: All the valley was shaded except for the far bend of the river. The sun was shining there several hundred yards from where I stood, and the white sycamores framed that sunshine, making it seem like a kind of portal, a cave of light, magnetic and warm. The woods seemed complete to me, the golden branches not less than summer green, sufficient, glowing, welcoming. As I walked, I realized that, for that moment, I needed nothing else.

1997: The sky plain gray. At 8:45 a.m., crows circled the back trees. A cardinal and chickadee called on High Street. The snow from two days ago remained on the ground, mottled with holes of warmer spaces in the yard. The air was quiet and mild, temperature in the high 20s. By noon: an edge to the cold, sharper, piercing. The sky brightened a little, sun showing through, then dull gray returned. When I jogged downtown just after lunch, the bite remained in the air. This afternoon, the wind picked up, the barometer dropping, the day becoming more fluid. Tonight the grass has a coating of ice, gossamer-like, crisp. The half moon flickers through the clouds. The barometer continues to fall.

1998: The morning chorus of starlings and sparrows seems strong to me this year; I walked out at nine o,clock to go to the doctor, and the air was full of birdsong.

2000: Camel cricket in the greenhouse this morning.

2005: Six inches of snow overnight, the roads slick. The last black Osage and mock orange leaves, torn from their branches by the storm, lie across the white yard. The temperature has not risen above freezing all month.

2006: Miami Beach to Brunswick, Georgia. Driving from temperatures of 70 degrees north through showers into the clear sky and cold of the Arctic high-pressure system that dominates the eastern half of the country. Wildflowers, white, yellow, violet noticed throughout the drive, the white most common.

And so there is an overlap not only in the foliage of deciduous trees (in which autumn extends longer and longer down the peninsula of Florida until it is swallowed up in the summer of the tropics) but also in the flowering of weeds, the persistence of which pushes up against the end of the year's northern perennial cycles, holding on at the edge of the winter until the Earth tilts just enough to allow new cycles to begin and spread spring toward Canada once again. Within the ambivalent fields and woods between North and South, fall and winter, November and February, lie the markers of a moveable frontier in both space and time, signatures of an elusive netherland from which the mysterious Christ of spring never fails to rise.

2008: A cloudy day with a south wind; heavy rain is predicted for tomorrow morning. The light covering of snow receded slowly through the night. The pond heater, which I put in yesterday, opened up the water, and I could see the fingerling koi swimming around.

2009: Mild today, then wind and rain as I left the store at 5:30. I walked to church after supper, high on a rum and coke, loved the story of the Immaculate Conception, loved the wind and the rain even more.

2012: Patricia Dewees writes: "Hello Bill, I just want to report in on seeing and hearing sandhill cranes in the sky above the South Glen on Saturday, December 8th. It was a thrill as I've only seen them in South Texas before this."

2014: Robins still calling in the neighborhood. Ed Oxley called: His snowdrops are just starting to push up through the mulch. Between Washington D.C. and Maine, another Nor'easter tonight.

2015: Robins still whinny off and on. The koi rise for food, the mild December keeping the water close to 50 degrees. In the hellebore bed, the first new bud has formed on the fresh, pale green foliage.

2016: The coldest weather of the year's second half is coming in today with wind and flurries. The final leaves of the backyard Osage clatter down until the branches are all bare. Along Elm Street, the dry flower petals of the hydrangeas shake in the west wind. Two purple iris stood twisted into themselves, frozen. The pond water is at 35 degrees, the fish suspended motionless just above the bottom. I moved the pond pump deeper to keep it away from the colder shore. I finished digging Bella's grave in the north garden, the ground still soft. Snow flakes falling outside my window now, just a few more and faster than the Osage leaves.

2017: At the solstice poetry reading tonight, Betty told me that she saw migrating flocks of cedar waxwings swarming at the honeysuckle berries, and golden-crowned kinglets, too. I told her I hadn't seen them, and she said I should get out more.

2019: As I stacked firewood this morning, robins were clucking and peeping all around. A cardinal called once in a while. Cirrus clouds thickened toward noon, rain and chill on the way.

Everything is beautiful in its season; and there is a beauty in every season of the year. God has for wise ends appointed the succession of summer and winter. The fruitfulness of the earth, and the health of man are consulted thereby. The cold of the winter purifies the air.... And the snow, produced by the cold, not only waters the earth, but cherishes it, and makes it to bring forth.

William Cooper, "A Winter Sermon," 18th Century

December 9th
The 343rd Day of the Year

There are afternoons in late autumn or early winter, during that recessive period of the year when the sun is low in the southern sky, when a special kind of light lies on the face of the familiar marshes. Snow has not yet fallen, or has thawed and gone, the land is brown, dun-colored, grey, with every vestige of the vernal seasons vanished save only for the tight buds on the maples. But in this very drabness...the sunlight lingers; it falls at an angle which invests every blade and seed-head with a life it has at no other time...it sheds a mellow tan effulgence, so that for a few hours of every afternoon, warm or cold, the meadows and the marshes seem endowed with a special kind of sentience in the soft sienna haze which holds to everything as were it the tangibility of sunlight itself.

August Derleth

Sunrise/set: 7:45/5:10
Day's Length: 9 hours 25 minutes
Average High/Low: 41/26
Average Temperature: 34
Record High: 65 – 1897
Record Low: - 7 – 1917

The Daily Weather
Today is one of the coldest and sunniest days of the first part of December, with highs remaining in the 20s more often than on any day so far this season (25 percent of the time). The absence of clouds does allow highs to warm into the 50s twenty percent of all the years; 40s happen 25 percent of the time, 30s thirty percent. Precipitation: 35 percent of the years, with odds 50/50 for snow or rain.

The Natural Calendar
Most second flowering of forsythia is finished. But new curly dock is often growing back in the wetlands. The freshest spears can be picked and used for salad greens, or sautéed with onions and maybe a small piece of bacon.

59

Woodchuck Hibernating Season and Bat Hibernating Season take place throughout southwestern Ohio. Redpoll Season arrives in the Northeast, and Mistletoe Gathering Season and Brown Pelican Nesting Seasons commence along the Gulf of Mexico.

Sandhill Crane Migrating Season (listen for them flying high overhead) passes through the region as December arrives. Crow Gathering Season approaches as thousands of crows congregate to spend the winter, their advent announced by the conclusion of Witch Hazel Flowering Season, by Beech Tree Shedding Season, New England Aster Foliage Yellowing Season, the Season of Orange Euonymus Berries (their white outer shells falling away in the cold), early Bulb Forcing Season, Christmas Tree Harvest Season, and the final cabbage butterfly of Cabbage Butterfly Season.

Daybook

1984: North Glen, snow on the ground, 50 degrees: Leafcup burned by severe cold, dock and dame's rocket prostrate. Garlic mustard peeks out around the snow mounds. Buds of the maples prominent, seed wings still hanging from the box elders. Ice on the quiet sloughs.

1985: Covered Bridge, 45 degrees and sunny. I was out taking photographs along the river. New rose leaves and skunk cabbage have emerged. Starlings whistling. A honey found drowned in the backwaters. Sedum, sweet Cicely growing back. Heard what I thought was a whip-poor-will toward Middle Prairie. Crocus spears have come up by the dooryard garden wall.

1987: A cardinal sang at 8:45 this morning. At the mill habitat, second-spring foliage holds its own in a mild, dry, fall and Early Winter. Even after a week of rain, the river has remained a foot below normal. I scouted for fishing holes, found the channel that I had missed at Far Hole during the summer. As I reached the dam, a beaver dove off the bank and swam upstream, its tail flapping up and down. Birds quiet in the woods, but at home, sparrows and starlings were chanting as though it were the middle of February.

1988: Lone robin seen at Middle Prairie, sitting near rose hips in the black and white field. The aloe plants are flowering in the greenhouse: a link to the tropics.

1997: Gray again today, the barometer continuing to fall steadily. Light mist of snow this morning. Intermittent chirping of a sparrow somewhere down the block, otherwise quiet - except for the cars on Dayton Street and the distant hum of the freeway traffic. This afternoon: melting, and the grass suddenly dominates the yard, which was covered with snow when I woke up. In the south garden, ice collapses over the deeper end of the pond. Fog tonight. In the flashlight beam, my breath and the mist are the same.

2003: The river is high at the mill. Red honeysuckle berries hold on above the water.

2004: Turkey vultures still here, six reported along the bike path today. They have stayed so long this year.

2005: Large raccoon caught in the attic. How he entered is still a mystery.

2006: Brunswick, Georgia to Newport, Tennessee. I noticed more leaves on the oaks and sweet gums as we drove north today. Leafdrop is definitely not over along the coast, and I wonder at the narrow gap between fall and spring in a location such as Savannah or Jacksonville. Is it a month or maybe just a few weeks? Could it be as little as a few days? Does just a flickering space exist between seasons at the southern frontier, a miniscule, shadowy hinge of time, a fulcrum as small as a single plant or a single hour?

2007: The forsythia leaves are gone now, but the Japanese honeysuckle foliage remains. Violet coralberries, orange bittersweet berries, red honeysuckle berries, blue privet berries stand out along the sidewalk toward Limestone Street. Rain began about ten o'clock, the day wet and dreary, birds waiting to feed until the weather turns, snow melting, patches of spring grass emerging in the lawn and along the roadsides. No goldfinches seen for several weeks. Tat in Madison says her finches have disappeared, too.

2009: Hard wind and rain before dawn, then the clouds went east and the half moon came out. We stayed in the barometric trough for three hours, then the wind blew hard, and Early Winter arrived. No crows heard the past couple of mornings, but the sparrows are feeding heavily before tomorrow's cold. Saw Casey at the bank – he said he saw nine buzzards yesterday, only one today.

2010: Ed Oxley called to say a friend of his had seen sandhills flying southeast on today.

2011: Massive flock of starlings seen on the back road to the mall, filling the trees and fields, swooping and swirling.

2012: Today, once again, a large flock of starlings in the High Street area, settling in the trees for a while, then moving to another block, then coming back.

2016: Deep cold moves in, perhaps for the rest of the winter. Only a few crinkled Osage leaves stay on their branches, the ground covered yellow-green with yesterday's leafdrop. There is a thin layer of ice on the pond for the first time, the fishes quiet beneath its transparent coverlet. I covered Bella in her grave this morning, the dug earth hard on top, a frozen crust that gave way when I brought the dirt over her with the hoe.

2017: The pond, about three-fourths covered with ice, is white with the first real snow of the winter. Coming home from Cincinnati, I saw five large flocks of starlings crossing above the highway. No sandhill crane sightings reported so far this year except for John Whitmore's on November 7th.

> Hear next of winter, when the florid summer,
> The bright barbarian scarfed in a swathe of flowers,
> The corn a golden ear-ring on her cheek,
> Has left our north to winter's finer etching,
> To raw-boned winter, when the sun
> Slinks in a narrow and a furtive arc,
> Red as the harvest moon, from east to west,
> And the swans go home at dusk to the leaden lake
> Dark in the plains of snow.

Vita Sackville-West

December 10th
The 344th Day of the Year

Winter by the fire. Outside, the rain
Becomes mist, then fog, then sleet.
Great husbandman, I think about your fields.
How well you make them, Lord.

Antonio Machado

Sunrise/set: 7:46/5:10
Day's Length: 9 hours 24 minutes
Average High/Low: 41/26
Average Temperature: 33
Record High: 67 – 1971
Record Low: - 9 – 1958

The Daily Weather
Today's average high temperature distribution: 50s thirty percent of the time, 40s just five percent, 30s forty-five percent, 20s twenty percent. Chances of precipitation are a little higher than yesterday's chances: 40 percent today, odds even for snow or rain. Clouds dominate the days more than half the time.

The Natural Calendar
The second week of December brings Duck Migration Season and Honeysuckle Leafdrop Season to a close along the 40th Parallel. For ducks on the northern Atlantic seaboard, the Season of Movement to Coastal Waters starts as ice covers inland ponds and lakes.

The Stars
Behold Orion rise,
His arms extended measures half the skies.
Manilius
Directly overhead at 10:00 p.m., Perseus stands below the North Star. In front of Perseus, to the west, find Andromeda, and then the Great Square. East of Perseus is Capella, the brightest star of the

Milky Way (except for Sirius in the far southeast),

By midnight, the Pleiades and Taurus will have replaced Perseus overhead, and Orion will be fully visible behind them. Regulus, the planting star of spring, will be just starting to come up along the eastern tree line.

At five o'clock in the morning, the Milky Way, along with winter's Orion and Sirius, the Dog Star, will be setting in the far west. Regulus will be overhead. Arcturus, the star that favors the seeding of squash and tomatoes will be the most prominent light in the east, and the pointers of the Big Dipper will be positioned almost exactly north-south.

Daybook

1982: Forsythia is still blooming in Mrs. Lawson's yard on High Street.

1983: Only an occasional forsythia leaf holds on now. The winter garden broccoli and kale are still strong. Red raspberries keep some purple leaves.

1988: South Glen, cloudy, windy, 31 degrees. Goldenrod, aster and wingstem seeds are about three-fourths gone. Some of the fallen leaves have already turned winter gray. Coralberries still hold, red orange.

1997: It started to rain about 11:00 last night, and the morning is soft and wet, in the low 40s. A crow came through before breakfast. The ice has dissolved in the pond, and all the snow has disappeared around the edges. The ground is soggy and slippery. When the clouds cleared for a moment a little while ago, a cardinal sang in the west woods. In the garden, the kale is deteriorating quickly. I should pick the last leaves for supper. Mid morning: starlings whistle in the back trees. A chickadee chatters. Another cardinal sings: they like the gentle weather and the rain. I turned on the pond pump; the waterfall, finally unfrozen, began to run. Another crow at 10:00. A few pansies are still blue by the pond. November and December have been dark this year, only scattered sun since the 19th of last month.

2000: Susi's spirea leaves hold at maybe half, rusted but hardy. Her

Osage leaves hang on, too, but they are brown and dry. The ice and snow have broken the ironweed in her back yard.

2002: The ground has been frozen for several days now, and there has been ice on the pond ever since December 3rd. Only twittering sounds from the birds in the woods. The mid-November revival of cardinal song is over.

2003: Rain and silence today. Snow moves across Wisconsin. The barometer drops below 29.40 as the December 11th cold front approaches. Only the Japanese honeysuckle leaves hold across the front hedge.

2004: A cardinal sang long and hard this morning a little after 7:30. In South Glen, the river was high after an all-day rain yesterday. Red euonymus berries lay about the ground. All the honeysuckle berries were gone, just a few of the pale green honeysuckle leaves left. No robins seen or heard. Moss was growing thick and sending up its delicate stalks. Patches of thin wild onions, covered with dew, glowed blue-green.

2006: Leaving the antidote of my fireside, I went looking for physic, a fresh signature, in the woods. I came across a small pool surrounded by bare saplings, a pond in a glade. It reminded me of the flooded field I played in as a boy one April, reminded me, too, of so many beaches and dreams.

   In these moods of mine, nothing is ever what it appears to be be; one thing becomes the sign of the other. Like children playing the game of telephone, I dialogue with myself until my thoughts come full circle, transformed into something completely different from the image that began the conversation.

   Later, I was driving to Washington Court House through the fog. I settled back in the truck and watched the countryside, looked out at the gray, still farm ponds. And the ponds became transformed to something else: the morning's perfect glade, an experience in the phosphorescent sea in 1960. An entire tapestry passed through my brain, guided only by a freeway landscape that transcended the modernity and speed of the vehicle in which I was driving, bonding me to the words and acts I had known and lost and now regained.

Once, before the time of freeways, I drove east through the Great Smoky Mountains in the rain, winding through the night, holding my breath at each curve, until I finally emerged onto the broad flatlands of South Carolina. Ahead of me lay sunrise and the coastal plain, the treacherous hills gone, the way made straight. Everything seemed now within my grasp.

Of course, that feeling of freedom and possibility led to something else: excitement tied to the romance of the road, the prospect of a promised land, a far castle like a mountain of the Lord. Like the fruit that tortured Tantalus, however, the horizon and its treasure receded in front of me. The incompletion and the hollowness became something like the "no-mind" of Zen, an absence, a vacuum filled only with koan.

Today, the recollections around me here are dendrites extending from within and from without, pulling me deeper into their tangles. The pond and the glade and the highway are sanctuaries for a moment, perfect and satisfying, but then they always take me somewhere else.

2007: Walking in the alley this morning about 9:30 with Bella, I heard the first cardinal that I've heard in a long time – one call, then the only sounds were the cackling of the starlings somewhere off towards downtown. This is another mild, gray day with rain before sunup and more melting. The snow of last week is almost gone, and the spring-like feeling of a few days ago has disappeared along with the first taste of thaw.

2008: No bird sounds this morning except for the crows before 8:00. In the alley, the red winterberries have begun to fall, another step to spring.

2009: Crows calling before 8:00 a.m. Deep cold came in last night, and the last of the snow flurries. Now the sun has come out; to the east, nothing but sunlight and high pressure. Two huge crows landed in the back yard at 9:45, scaring away the sparrows and chickadees.

In Madison, Wisconsin, my sister Tat reports: "We're

buried!" Rae was here last night and we tucked in by the fire, indeed - she kept turning the back light on to watch the snow fall (and fall, and fall -- if the driveway's any measure, I'm betting we had 24 inches of wet, heavy snow). This morning we went out and shoveled (and shoveled, and shoveled); a couple of lovely neighbors came and gave us a hand; we came in and are making cranberry bread and cookies to take around to them. Mighty nice day!"

2010: Thousands of starlings swarming and swooping as I reached the freeway south this morning on my way to Cincinnati.

2011: The full December moon set in the west-northwest this morning about 6:30.

2012: A cardinal sang while I was standing by the fireplace this morning at 7:30 sharp. And most every morning for the past week, I have found camel crickets on the brick wall by near the couch when I turned on the light at about 6:15.

2013: Home from Oregon to find six inches of snow, last of the Zelcova and Osage leaves lying on top.

2016: Across southwestern Ohio, only a few patches of pale green honeysuckle leaves give color to the landscape. At home, temperature in the teens darkens the Japanese honeysuckles foliage and withers the forsythia. The sandhill cranes came in on schedule last week! John B. had predicted they would follow the first severe cold front of Early Winter south toward the Gulf. Indeed they did.

Moya saw them first on Saturday, the 10th, "about noonish," she estimated, as she was crossing at the BP crosswalk. "I heard a sound, and it wasn't a goose sound. I looked up and saw them in a 'V'. They were higher than geese fly, it seemed to me, and they came in from the north, made a gentle turn over Yellow Springs and then headed toward Xenia. I counted 20 in half of the 'V' so there must have been about 40 in all. And I've been waiting and looking for them for 43 years, and I kept hearing about them and reading about them in the paper, and I asked myself if I would ever see them for myself, and then I did!"

John called to say that Doug from Beachmont Organics

north of Spring Valley heard cranes about six o'clock yesterday evening flying in low near his farm, maybe landing. Doug said that although he often sees them high above his property, this is the first time they've come in so low.

2017: An inch of the first snow by daybreak.

The speculations, intuitions, and formal ideas we refer to as "mind" are a set of relationships to the interior landscape with purpose and order; some of these are obvious, many impenetrably subtle. The shape and character of these relationships in a person's thinking, I believe, are deeply influenced by where on this earth one goes, what one touches, the patterns one observes in nature – the intricate history of one's life in the land, even a life in the city, where wind, the chirp of birds, the line of a falling leaf, are known. These thoughts are arranged further, according to the thread of one's moral, intellectual, and spiritual development. The interior landscape responds to the character and subtlety of an exterior landscape; the shape of the individual mind is affected by land as it is by genes.

Barry Lopez, *Crossing Open Ground*

Over the woodlands brown and bare,
Over the harvest-fields forsaken,
Silent, and soft, and slow
Descends the snow.

Henry Wadsworth Longfellow

Sunrise/set: 7:46/5:10
Day's Length: 9 hours 24 minutes
Average High/Low: 40/25
Average Temperature: 33
Record High: 65 – 1894
Record Low: - 8 – 1917

The Daily Weather
More than half the years, highs remain in the 30s; sometimes, they even fall to the 20s (five percent of the time). But a rare afternoon above 60 was recorded in 1978 and in 2020, and 65 is the record high from 1894. Other benign possibilities: 15 percent chance of mild 50s and 15 percent for 40s. Skies are overcast 50 percent of the years, but snow falls only one year out of five, and rain only one in ten.

The Natural Calendar
Seed companies have begun to sell their corn and soybeans for seed now, and discounts are often available to farmers for early purchases.

Daybook
1988: River low at South Glen, no chubs or shiners bite. If I hadn't seen the schools of carp at Far Hole a few weeks ago, I would think the water dead.

1991: Carolina wren eating seeds in the coreopsis.

1992: Gray skies since the end of October. Feeding the birds gives me some relief from my seasonal affective disorders. Are the birds unaffected by the solar retreat? Or they simply know how to deal with it: be outside and eat!

1996: Downtown at 6:50 this morning: sky dark, warm wind from the south, the temperature above 50 degrees. When I got out of the car, all I could hear was the boisterous chatter of a huge flock of sparrows above me in the pear trees.

1997: More pale gray, the ninth gray day in a row. The air is crisp, though, sharpened by the arrival of a high-pressure system overnight. The wind is still now, and the land seems to be settling down solidly into winter.

2000: All the leaves have fallen, the canopy gone, the sky open and the air still. The blue river beside me seems like the border of my life. The year is over, and I stand in the eye of this afternoon, feeling complete in what I am and what I have been and seen here.

2002: Sleet falling steadily today. The bamboo along the south wall droops down under the weight of the ice. A skunk was run over last night on Dayton-Yellow Springs Road.

2004: A pileated woodpecker called in the backyard this afternoon. When I went out to try to find it, it flew off toward Greg's yard.

2007: Gray and mild, light mist: Walking this morning with Bella, I saw a small brown moth fluttering at the rugged bark of Mateo's ancient elm tree. As I worked in the attic, another brown moth came beating at my light. Outside this afternoon, the high reached 64 degrees in the soft south wind.

2008: Walking through the alley this morning with Bella, I heard and saw a small flock of robins moving through the maples. And in locust trees behind our yard, starlings were singing for the first time in what seems like weeks. On a walk with Jeff at the Indian Mound Park later in the morning: We disturbed a large murder of crows in the pine forest there. A freak snowstorm this afternoon has dropped eight inches of snow on New Orleans.

2009: At 12:50, Kathryn called to say she had just seen a flock of sandhill cranes flying over High Street. She heard them, went outside and looked up to see the sunlight coming through their wings. At 2:30, Aida called to say she had seen the same flock over near her house around the same time as Kathryn.

2011: Cold and clear today, the pond frozen over. Birds feeding heavily, a cowbird seen for the first time this winter. John Blakelock wrote: "Saw cranes today, about 12:35 p.m., two "V" shaped formations flying in tandem, 25-30 per flock, chortling and bugling as they passed."

2014: Jon Whitmore called to report he saw sandhill cranes crossing over John Bryant Park at around 9:30 and around 2:30. He also said he had seen two other flocks, one a few weeks ago flying over Jacoby Creek, and another almost a month ago.

2015: Warm days and nights continue. Robins still whinnying off and on. New waterleaf growing up among the euonymus leaves downtown. The lawns beside Dayton-Yellow Springs Road have numerous dandelion heads gone to seed. Downtown, a privet bush is budding.

2017: As I talked to Audrey in the greenhouse, a hawk floated down to wait for prey at the backyard bird feeder. How long did Audrey and I talk before it attacked? Maybe half an hour, then it dropped suddenly onto a bird or vole and then flew off. Then sparrows, chickadees and cardinals returned almost immediately, the danger sated, life and death as usual.

2018: Hundreds of geese feeding in the field across from Ellis Pond. At the oak grove, the sawtooth oak and the swamp chestnut oak keep their brittle leaves. The cypress trees are surrounded by their rust-colored needles, very little foliage remaining.

2020: A rare, soft day with a high of 62 (after two in the 50s), and I finished work on the greenhouse wall, repaired rotting sills, cleaned the fishpond filter, cleared one garden plot for daffodils. Before dawn, the fourth-quarter crescent moon was leading Venus out of the east through cirrus wisps of pink and gold. This afternoon, Jill and I drove beneath an undulating flock of blackbirds that stretched from east to west across the village. Tonight, small moths at the porch light.

We sat there and thought about how much colder it was yet to become. It was a strong and scary feeling knowing that it, the great cold, lay out there in the future, in the dark, a certainty.

Rick Bass

December 12th
The 346th Day of the Year

I climbed down the face of the cliff, which would age in the freeing and thawing of another winter. I climbed past the crevice in which the ladybugs slept. I passed by the spider that had spun a bag of silk as armor against the oncoming cold. The moisture on the surfaces of the rocks had begun to freeze, and they were slippery. I climbed down through the edge of another winter.

Paul Gruchow

Sunrise/set: 7:47/5:10
Day's Length: 9 hours 23 minutes
Average High/Low: 40/25
Average Temperature: 33
Record High: 69 – 2015
Record Low: - 3 – 1960

The Daily Weather
Highs in the 60s occur five percent of the years, 50s twenty percent, 40s twenty percent, 30s thirty percent, 20s twenty-five percent. A morning below zero comes once every decade. Clouds cover the sky half the years. Chances of precipitation: 30 percent, with rain four times as common as snow.

The Natural Calendar
Bedding Plant Season starts at new moon time in Early Winter; now is the time to prepare seeds and flats for May flowers and vegetables. This season peaks again at the new moon in January, February and March.

Daybook
1983: One dandelion still blooms in the lawn. At South Glen, milkweed pods are black and empty, coming apart. Large hawk seen along Corry Street.

1985: The late summer plants I brought inside before the frost have died: marigolds, zinnias, impatiens. Winter insects, the whiteflies, mealy bugs, some spider mites have taken them all.

1987: Red-tailed hawk seen on the way to Wilberforce.

1989: Geese fly over 8:27 a.m. Forsythia leaves brown, many holding on. Japanese honeysuckle still deep green, almost like mistletoe.

1990: Covered Bridge habitat, 60 degrees, partly cloudy: The water was slow and clear, as low as I've seen it in winter. After a week of sunny, warm weather, hemlock was spreading up over the brittle sycamore leaves. Skunk cabbage was green in the swamp. There was new columbine foliage on the cliff, and one miterwort all grown back. Aster leaves were two inches long, and sedum thick. Ragwort had developed most quickly of all. The wind sounded like the ocean on the ridge above me. From the high path, the river was so bright winding through the valley. At home, a dandelion was flowering in the lawn. In the greenhouse, one tomato vine was at eight feet, fruits from all the plants coming in, as much as we can eat.

1993: Covered Bridge: Robins seen along the river. They must be planning to stay the winter.

1995: The year seems to pause as the sun reaches to within a few minutes of solstice, but natural history continues to be the sum of observations. Since there is no limit to what a person might watch and record, stasis is only in the eye of the beholder. Like every other season, winter accumulates, is the product of the sensations it causes, is only what we see it to be, is all that we see it to be.

1997: Yesterday to Springfield: Crows in the cornfields, in the trees and flying back and forth over the stores. There seems to be nothing unique that brings them to this urban setting, no unusual food supply or cover. Their convention must go back in history for hundreds or thousands of years. It always excites me to see them here. They reassure me that the world is still turning the way it should, in spite of the pollution, and global warming, overpopulation. This morning, the barometer is up, and the sun finally broke through. The solid pale gray of the sky was replaced by blue. Everything changed. But then by two o'clock, the clouds returned.

2002: Two sparrow hawks seen on the wires near Archbold, a hundred miles north of Yellow Springs.

2007: Crows pass through after sunrise. Starlings watch the neighborhood from Don's tree. Sparrows cluster in our forsythia bushes and wait for me to feed them.

2008: No cardinals heard all month. New England is paralyzed by an ice storm. Full moon and perigee brought snow and ice from Texas to Maine.

2009: Just before noon, Casey called to report sandhill cranes. They were circling over his property, he said, maybe 400 feet above the water, so close he could see the sun through their wings, circling and circling, 75 to 100 birds, hanging in a bunch wheeling around and around, for maybe five or six minutes.

Then just as I hung up, Jeanie pulled up in front of our house, came running in: "Sandhill cranes!" she cried, and I went out and there they were, calling and circling. And then we saw a smaller group approach the circle, and only when that group got close did the larger flock move on south. A few minutes later, Ruth Paige called; she had seen a flock about the same time along the bike path. And she had seen her first sandhill cranes about six years ago, she said (December 7, 2013 to be exact), at almost the same location. Then at 1:40 this afternoon, Jeanie and I heard more cranes; I ran outside and saw a great flock disappearing into the southwest over the back locust trees.

Ruth has lived in Yellow Springs 20 years and has only had those two sightings. Casey grew up here and spent most of his life here, and he never remembers seeing the cranes until just the past few years.

And Matt Minde wrote: "I saw them myself on Saturday (the 12th), around 11 a.m., about 40–50, circling above Mills Lawn School, then later a huge flock of them — perhaps 80 or so — flying over Casey's old place (where we live now). Incredible!"

2012: Crows at exactly 7:40 this morning. At Ellis Pond, a very thin coating of ice on sections of the water.

2014: John Whitmore reported another flock of cranes heading south over Dayton-Yellow Springs Road.

2015: Rick reported a small snake in his pond hunting frogs today. He also said he watched large flocks of robins, hundreds of them, he said, flying over his property, heading west. Today's high of 69 degrees set a new record. And I heard a screech owl as I walked back from Jill's about midnight.

2016: As the barometer drops before the next cold wave, the temperature rises into the upper 30s, the fish respond sluggishly to a small feeding. On the front sidewalk, bittersweet beginning to fall.

2017: It had been a disappointing month. Where were the sandhill cranes? John W. thought he heard them in the night of November 7, but no one else reported seeing or hearing them until today.

The morning was cloudy and full of snowbursts, the afternoon sunny. It was bitter cold throughout the day, wind from the northwest, the barometer rising as another winter front came through. And then the great flocks came.

Like on December 12 of 2016, Jon W was the first to call, this year at 12:41 in the afternoon (instead of 10:30 in the morning last year): "I think it was sandhill cranes," he said, "that particular sound. I couldn't see them, but it had to be them."

Then at 2:00, he called again, this time with even better, more definite news, the hesitancy of the earlier message gone: "Here they are," he said, "about thirty of them, circling overhead, seeming to drift south, then moving back north again, just floating along."

Then Ben reported: "I wanted to let you know I saw two groups of sandhill cranes above the Glen today, just south of the Yellow Spring and Birch Creek confluence flying southwest at 1:45 p.m."

About 2:20, Betty called from Bryant Park Road to say that she had seen a great flock of at least fifty heading to the southeast, and that she had seen them first about 1:30 when she was walking along the river.

Rick was watching, too: "Between 2:00 and 2:20 today I

saw several flocks of sand hill cranes flying south over the west end of the Village," he wrote. There were around sixty in the first group and another later flock of roughly a hundred birds-all chirping and chatting among themselves."

John Blakelock also saw them about 2:45 close to the gravel pits off near Enon, "a group of maybe 40 or 50."

About the same time, Maureen called to tell me she had seen sandhill cranes flying south over Antioch College. And the flock kept coming: Paul called at 3:45 to say he also saw that flock over the village. Then Ann called to say she had also twenty or thirty of them over the Glen at 4:15. She called back three-quarters of an hour later to report another sighting, "probably forty going south." And Jill saw them at 5:07.

So the sandhill cranes passed above us throughout the afternoon into the dark, wave after wave, sometimes pausing overhead to circle, perhaps waiting for others to catch up.

I thought about my experience one spring at the Platte River watching thousands of sandhill cranes assemble in the evening for their journey north, and then in the morning, as I drove southeast, I encountered what seemed an endless series of formations moving back toward the river. They kept flying toward me as I drove into daybreak, their mutating patterns always coming west, filling the sky to my right and to my left. The Sun rose deep scarlet, filtered and softened through altostratus, so I could watch the black, rippling swoops of cranes against it, and I drove on toward Grand Island, below thirty miles of them advancing to their meeting place.

I couldn't help but think that, on December 12, Yellow Springs had been able encounter a similar or even greater flock, a flock so vast that it took the entire afternoon to fly above us, and that with the sightings from so many people, we were able to give witness to the immensity of what was happening.

2018: The Osage fruits are dark now, mud green, ochre, but still pale green inside when the squirrels tear them apart. Up the street, the fallen leaves from Rachel's ginkgo tree have turned all rusty brown. Bittersweet berries are thinning quickly.

Without solar, stellar, floral and meteorological pointers, there would be no recognizable seasons. In the same way, perception of place is dependent upon an ordered collection of familiar objects. Time and space move in or out of focus, depending on the texture, odor, color, position, number and sequence of the markers that guide us. These markers also link perception to story, creating an inseparable connection between internal and external worlds, between markers and consciousness, and between one consciousness and another.

Leon Quel

December 13th
The 347th Day of the Year

Now groane the Zephers;
Poplars shudder, naked
Like the Ears of Asses
Prophesying Storms and Snow.
Now Beasties roll about
And frolick in the Face
of gloomy Times!

Columenus

Sunrise/set: 7:48/5:10
Day's Length: 9 hours 22 minutes
Average High/Low: 40/25
Average Temperature: 32
Record High: 66 – 1901   (65 – 2015)
Record Low: - 6 – 1960

The Daily Weather
Five percent of December 13ths are in the 50s or 60s, twenty-five percent in the 40s, fifty percent in the 30s, twenty percent in the 20s or teens. Precipitation, frequently in the form of snow, occurs 30 percent of the time. Skies are clear to partly cloudy a little more than half of the days. Lows drop below freezing all but 20 percent of the nights.

The Natural Calendar
Between today and January 3rd, normal average temperatures in the Lower Midwest drop one degree every four days instead of one degree every three, starting a reversal of the rapid onset of winter cold. The averages remain steady throughout most of the year's first month; on January 28th they begin to rise.

The Shooting Stars
Late in the second week of December, the Geminid meteors arrive out of the northern heavens near Castor and Pollux, the twins of

Gemini, to the upper left of giant Orion. Several days after the Geminids, the Ursid Meteors fly out from the Little Dipper, a small constellation just to the east of the North Star.

Most folk stories about shooting stars complement the notion of a Thin Time at the transition between late autumn and Early Winter, a time during which the barriers become more fragile between those living on this side of death and those on the other side. Such a spiritual aura around the meteoric prelude to winter solstice offers a secular mystique to the season of darkness, easily blending with religious liturgies that enhance awareness of the close of the old year and the coming of the new.

Meteoric events were thought to be, in the words of William Ashworth Jr., "trans-factual." Ashworth noted that people found in their occurrence a "higher truth, the truth of the miraculous." Hanukkah, the Jewish festival of lights, and Christian Christmas with its star of wonder, dovetail easily with the appearance of December's meteors, follow the shooting starlight with hopeful and celebratory ceremonies which humans often use to face the cold and gloom of the months past solstice.

Daybook

1982: Ice has formed at the edges of Massey Creek, and the Little Miami. Grinnell swamp is frozen over.

1984: Trip east to Washington DC: Landscape uniformly dun, gray skies throughout the drive.

1989: Early Winter continues with a jerky but steady motion, getting gradually stronger since the 8th.

1992: Cardinal sings at 8:35 a.m. Grayness for weeks now, bleak, wet weather; even the barometric high of 30.42 today produces no sun, and I feel an oppression, the sky too low, pushing down on top of me.

1995: All the bittersweet hulls have fallen now from the vine on High Street; the orange. Berries still hold ten feet or so above the sidewalk.

1997: The sun has come out all the way now, and the wind is steady from the northwest, cumulus racing across the sky, low and tattered. I feel exhilarated, caught in the tide of this movement. At the same time, I feel unprepared, unused to so much sunlight and the absence of the dark clouds. But my lack of preparation makes no difference later: the sky becomes gray again by noon, stays overcast through the night.

1999: Around the yard, the leaves are matting down, their familiar shapes dissolving into the grass. I can't tell apples from white mulberries, or Osage orange from mock orange. The box elders have broken down completely, not a trace of them left. Instead of shedding the rain, now the leaves accept it, porous, allowing the season. Ferns, prostrate, cover and mulch the hostas.

2004: One buzzard sighting reported by Jeanie today.

2005: Bright sun and cold: A cardinal sang as I walked out the back door this morning at 9:30.

2006: Cardinal at 7:25 this morning. Under the bird feeders, a few snowdrops that had been pushing out of the ground have been trampled and shredded by the sparrows.

2007: Many bittersweet hulls and berries hold to their branches along Limestone Street.

2011: Honeysuckle berries no longer cluttering the front sidewalk, but a few hang on.

2012: Crows at 7:35 this morning. Six starlings whistling in the alley at 9:00. Same status of the honeysuckle berries as last year.

2013: Crows at 7:35 this morning. Clear skies, no frost on the windshields, big storm forecast for tonight.

2014: Robins frolicking in the woods at the St. Clare Monastery near Cincinnati. No cardinals heard these days, few starlings in the neighborhood.

2015: Steady robin twittering and whinnying through the morning. The mild days across the eastern half of the country have brought some cherry trees to bloom in Washington D.C.

2016: No cherry blossoms this year! Four inches of snow today (the first substantial snow of this winter) and lows in the single digits (also the first of the season) tonight.

2018: John Blakelock wrote that his friend, Lisa, "a hard-core birdwatcher, saw a group of 17 cranes, while driving on Far Hills Avenue in Dayton about 2:00 in the afternoon. She said they were very high, and in a 'V' formation, and heading toward the southwest." Lisa's sighting was about thirty miles west of Yellow Springs.

2020: As Jill and I walked in the gloom after sundown: a sizeable "V" of geese flew over honking, and in the distance a great cacophony of goose calls rose up to guide them to the night roost.

I came to realize clearly that mind is no other than mountains and rivers and the great wide earth, the sun and the moon and the stars.

Zen Master Dogen

December 14th
The 348th Day of the Year

Then for the teeming, quietest, happiest days of all!
The brooding and blissful halcyon days!

Walt Whitman

Sunrise/set: 7:49/5:11
Day's Length: 9 hours 22 minutes
Average High/Low: 40/25
Average Temperature: 32
Record High: 66 – 1901
Record Low: - 15 – 1898

The Daily Weather

Today's high temperature distribution: five percent chance of 60s, five percent for 50s, thirty percent for 40s, forty percent for 30s, ten percent for 20s, ten percent for teens. Double-digit below-zero morning temperatures enter the southwestern Ohio record books, but even single-digit below-zero dawns are rare, coming only five percent of the years. On this date, rain falls 25 percent of the days, snow just five percent.

The Natural Calendar

The Halcyon Days, a traditional two-week period of calm before the turbulence of winter, begin today. According to Greek legend, the halcyon (kingfisher) built its nest on the surface of the ocean and laid its eggs late in the fall. In order to ensure the brood would emerge safely, the bird calmed winds for a week before and after winter solstice.

On the other hand, the Season of Double-Digit Below-Zero Temperatures spans the period between December 14 and March 22 at average elevations along the 40th Parallel. Although such cold is relatively rare, each day in this three-month season carries up to a five-percent chance of a morning of -1 or below.

This week also brings the Season of the Shortest Days of the Year. The sun lies at its lowest point in the noon sky, and rises and sets at its farthest points south. Solar declination reaches 23 degrees, 26 minutes on December 21 and remains at that position on the 22nd and 23rd. But in Yellow Springs (and in much of the United States around this date), sunset time is a minute later today than on December 13th, and the Season of Later Sunset Times begins.

Daybook

1986: Crows following the river, moving north across the Springfield highway. Grackles cackle and flutter around the yard as though today were a day in spring. Geese heard flying over the village this afternoon.

1987: Patches of blue sky, then deep and lighter grays, broken apart in the rush of the wind, the front gate broken in the gusts, speckled starlings calmly working the lawn. Long flock of crows seen moving across the road along the old railroad bed north.

1992: This is the tenth day in a row without sun, and there have been almost no clear skies since the end of October. The air is damp and sullen, carried by a huge high-pressure system that brings neither a change in temperature nor any clearing. Chopping wood, I found centipedes active under a large locust log.

1993: A pair of great blue herons flew over me upstream from the Covered Bridge this afternoon.

1997: Walking to church this morning, I watched large blotches of purple-gray in the clouds, mottling the overcast sky with giant pastel patches. On the way to Springfield this afternoon, I saw just one glimpse of sun and just a fragment of blue. Then at 9:20 this evening I went outside, the sky had cleared, the moon was full and bright!

2004: Blustery and cold with occasional snowbursts: Flocks of starlings feeding throughout the area as Jeanie and I did our Christmas shopping.

2005: I found a woolly-bear caterpillar crawling on the greenhouse floor this morning.

2006: Gentle weather, clear skies and 40s before dawn, warming to the middle 50s through the afternoon. A cardinal sang at 7:22 this morning. When I went outside around 8:00, more cardinal song.

2008: Crows at 8:00 this morning, windy, cloudy, mild. In the garden, the hydrangea heads are drooping, the Jerusalem artichokes have fallen over, the season of tipping stems begun. In the alley, the tall coneflower stalks have collapsed. Near the pond, the false boneset has broken, and the small white asters are leaning. Jeni in Portland, Oregon reports the city paralyzed by snow and ice.

2010: Crows heard at 8:15 this morning. Seven degrees at dawn and a half a foot of snow on the ground.

2011: Almost every morning these days, nuthatches are calling in the alley and along Stafford Street. Great flock of starlings blackening the trees in Byron. Buzzards seen on the road south.

2012: Three dandelions blooming in the south lawn, sun along Limestone Street, a robin peeping somewhere in the alley.

2013: All-day snow: Crows at 8:00, calling steadily for maybe ten minutes.

2014: Crows at 7:40 this morning, warm air from the Gulf moving up into the Dakotas, the November deep-cold high long gone. After several mild days here, the koi swim lazily around the pond, rise slowly to eat when I toss their food into the water.

2015: Algae returning to the pond after four days near or above 60 degrees. And Matt wrote: "I heard an actual lone cricket outside yesterday — December 13! That has got to be some sort of local record, as well as a testament to possibly the loneliest cricket in the region." From New Orleans, Jill sends a photo of a Monarch butterfly perched on a railing.

2016: Rick Walkee, 11:30 a.m., "I heard a sound I've never heard before. I've seen them before, but I've never heard them, their haunting sound, fabulous, fabulous call, I looked up and there they were. There were 25 of them, sandhill cranes, just yakking away having a real conversation. They were definitely headed south over High Street."

2017: Laura wrote and sent a photo of sandhill cranes flying over Spring Valley-Paintersville Rd. "This was the second group I saw around noon today," she said. "The first group was about twice this size. It was very exciting to see so many! As you might notice, this group seems to be disorganized. However, they were flying in a "V" and then they started circling, as if evaluating whether to land and take a rest. Then they came out of the circling behavior and went back in a V and continued south. Finally, when walking on the trail near the Glen around 5:00 p.m. I thought I heard some sandhills, but could not see them."

2019: Driving to and from Cincinnati: One vast flock of starlings, for an instant overshadowing the sky. Later a smaller but still sizeable flock. On Dayton-Yellow Springs Road, a skunk had been run over in the night, a casualty of the milder days. From the village, Leslie writes: "Starlings, qty 500 +- (=huge flock), squeaking & chattering in trees in our backyard and also around Talus Drive circle (for 2 hours, noon to 2 p.m.)."

If there are mountains, I look at mountains.
On rainy days, I listen to the rain.
Spring, summer, autumn, winter.
Tomorrow too will be good
Tonight too will be good.

Santoka Taneda (with Tara Marquez and Henry T)

December 15th
The 349th Day of the Year

Arrives the snow, and driving o'er the fields,
Seems nowhere to alight: the whited air
Hides the hills and woods, the river, and the heaven,
And veils the farm - house at the garden's end.

Ralph Waldo Emerson

Sunrise/set: 7:49/5:11
Day's Length: 9 hours 22 minutes
Average High/Low: 39/24
Average Temperature: 32
Record High: 63 – 1984
Record Low: - 10 – 1901

The Daily Weather

Highs in the 60s come five percent of the afternoons; 50s occur on ten percent, 40s on 35 percent, 30s on 40 percent, 20s on five percent, teens on five percent. Skies are cloudy half the time, and there is a ten-percent chance of a morning below zero. Snow falls one day in four, rain one in five. The deepest December cold spell in half a century began today in 1983. It lasted until the 31st. The following year, there were highs in the 60s on the 15th and 16th.

The Weather in the Week Ahead

The third week of December almost always brings in a strong cold wave between the 15th and the 17th, and if this front arrives on its earliest date, the 15th, expect another weather system on the 19th or 20th. The coldest December days, those with better than a 35 percent chance of temperatures in the 20s or below, all come at this time of year: the 17th, 18th, 19th, 25th, and 26th. The most bitter day this week in my weather history is the 19th, with a 30 percent chance of highs only in the teens. And more below-zero temperatures occur between the 18th and the 26th than on any other December mornings. Precipitation is common throughout the period, with every day this week bringing a 50 percent chance of rain or snow except December

87

16th, which is typically the driest and the sunniest day between now and Christmas. Double-digit below-zero temperatures are possible between December 15th and March 22nd in Yellow Springs.

The Natural Calendar

Across the Lower Midwest, the Season of Average Highs in the 30s begins on December 15th and persists through February 20th, bracketing almost exactly the three seasons of winter. Pruning Season gets underway as average highs drop into the 30s; it continues until the average highs climb once again past 40.

The Season of Gull Migration is usually over by December 16th, ending major Ohio bird migration activity. In the northern woods, White Ear Tuft Season marks the ears of red squirrels, and Wood Turtle Hibernation Season occurs along the rivers.

The Season of Slowing Cold takes place between this week and January 3rd, normal average temperatures dropping one degree every four days instead of one degree every three, signaling a slowdown in the chilling of the land. Soon the averages become steady; on January 28th they start to climb toward summer.

Daybook

1984: Record high temperatures in the 60s. Walking north along the railroad tracks, I saw a flicker and a small flock of robins, a few forsythia flowers.

1986: Jacoby: Paths still green, second-spring foliage strong. Ice along the brooks. Geese flew over in the late afternoon. Chubs took my bait, none caught.

1987: Storm, limbs down, sparrows singing in the howling wind.

1992: Jacoby Swamp, 55 degrees: Skunk cabbage a hand high but not open. Some of the hillsides green with garlic mustard. Long, flushed moss on fallen branches, brilliant red berries on the barberry. And blue in the streams from the sky, the flashing of sunlight on the water. Crows calling on the other side of the ridge, and chickadees and wrens chattering ahead of me in the swamp. A startled deer in the cattail tangle goes crashing toward the river. One winter robin whinny.

The pure springs that wander through the bottoms are

adorned with cress, dock, ragwort, buttercup and the brightest grass: oases of color and sound, never overcome by winter, never browned or dulled, almost never silenced. Water striders in the holding ponds above the river, half a dozen ruling a minute inland sea full of fallen leaves, and algae, surrounded by moss and foliage of sweet rockets, asters, and miterwort. Below the pool, where the water escapes, there is a wide and deep line of cress, like an artery of spring. Clump of orange fungi on the side of a dead tree. A little further down the path, a nut-brown button type toadstool with a short stem, growing from a rotten log. Thimble plant seeds have disappeared here. Staghorns still hold, blood red, and some pinecones. One tan moth flies across the brook down into the valley.

1993: Witch hazel still blooming along Dayton Street, no change from a month ago. The red crab apples are still as strong as when their leaves came down. Flowering kale doing fine even after temperatures down to 15 degrees.

1997: Finally clear skies. The moon setting at dawn. The sun rising orange in the southeast, the horizon clean, cloudless. Out on the freeway, the frozen grass, dull under the gray skies of last week, is tinted gold, all the browns of the fields made richer and deeper by the winter sunlight, the red buds on the maples glowing, the yellow willows shining. Hazy gray-blue horizon over the city. Geese flew over at 2:10 p.m. as I was writing this daybook entry.

2005: In the middle of an all-day snow, a fly emerged from somewhere in the house, landed on my computer screen at 2:22 p.m.

2006: Bella and I walked through the alley to the sound of starlings in the trees down the block.

2007: No starlings in the alley this morning, but a flock of crows flew over at about a quarter to eight. A major storm system is moving across the Midwest today – we already have three inches of snow on the ground at noon, and precipitation is expected to continue through tomorrow. Oklahoma and Missouri were shut down last week by ice storms, and they are getting hit again. Tat says Madison, Wisconsin, has almost two feet of snow on the ground. By evening, we have a break in the storm, and the snow has turned to slush. More snow is due after midnight, lasting until mid morning. One striped-breasted song sparrow seen beneath the feeder today.

2008: Most of the pear leaves downtown have fallen.

2010: The witch hazel leaves and the oakleaf hydrangea leaves contract and droop in the cold, and the Japanese honeysuckle foliage has darkened and curled. Across the South, cities are recording record low temperatures, and the fruit and vegetable crops may be ruined from deep frost.

2011: Rain for two days, steady south winds, highs near 60 today, buzzards seen sailing above the highway south to Xenia.

2014: Robins twittering and peeping around 8:00 this morning, a small flock of overwintering starlings in the trees by the Catholic church, crows back and forth.

2016: Deep cold throughout the day, low 7 degrees, high just in the teens. Ed Oxley reports from Miami County, about 30 miles northwest of Yellow Springs: " A flock of sandhill cranes, probably about 50 or so, flew over my place between 3:30 and 4:30 in the afternoon, heading southeast – and maybe toward Yellow Springs. I just want to let you now that the cranes are in the area."

2019: Today was chilly, but Ellis Pond was free of ice, and the snow was still a ways west of Ohio. The cranes, as is their custom, however, fly before the storm, and area residents were keeping I the afternoon, I walked out the door of my house on High Street, and John drove by then backed up and told me he had been chasing cranes just south of town. It had been a big flock, he said with a smile.

"Heard 'em first, quite clear, I thought they were low and close. When they finally appeared they were East of me, maybe 1500' up: 3 over-lapping "V"s with maybe 70 birds. I'd guess they were right in between us and Clifton," John told me.

I had just missed them.

At 3:30, Casey left a message that he had just seen "two

groups of those beautiful birds going over, probably fifty or sixty, headed due south, sort of following the bike path."

A little later, Jim Leonard and Ann Randolf reported they had witnessed the same event from Steward Street at the same time. Jim had recorded them, two smaller flocks seeming to go west, and then a large flock heading south. Ann had confirmed his suspicion: "They were sandhills!"

Audrey sent a note on Monday: "My husband and I heard and saw sandhill cranes yesterday! Two big vees fluidly twisting together into a single large vee, at least 30 birds in all. We were walking in front of Nipper's Corner, they were headed southwest--toward the river, we supposed. It was about 3:30 in the afternoon. They were flying low, call-rattling to each other. The glimpse was thrilling, moving, slightly unreal...."

And Cliff wrote, too, and included a video, taken that afternoon by a friend on Larkin Road, of a great, undulating formation of cranes that stretched from one side of the sky to the other, their sharp cries clearly audible above road noise.

Three inches of snow came in with the darkness, and the next day, more snow and wind and cold expected in the single digits.

2020: Cold 21 degrees with wind. Crows before sunrise, then a cardinal.

Leaving water, I turn uphill.
A squawk, I lift my gaze upon
four slim cranes, wings wide,
silent choir singing me deep, deeper.
All is not buried; I'm alive.

From "Depth" by Ed Davis

December 16th
The 350th Day of the Year

The simplicity of winter has a deep moral. The return of nature, after such a career of splendor and prodigality, to habits so simple and austere, is not lost upon either the head or the heart.

John Burroughs

Sunrise/set 7:50/5:11
Day's Length: 9 hours 21 minutes
Average High/Low: 39/24
Average Temperature: 32
Record High: 65 – 1984
Record Low: - 15 – 1951

The Daily Weather
Today's temperature distribution: five percent chance of 60s, fifteen for 50s, thirty-five percent for 40s, twenty percent for 30s, twenty percent for 20s. And for the first time this winter, there is a five to ten percent chance of a high only in the single digits. Morning temperatures fall below freezing all but 30 percent of the time, and below-zero temperatures occur one day in 20. Rain comes about 15 percent of the days, snow another 15 percent, but the 16th is one of December's brighter days, the sun appearing a full 70 percent of the time.

The Natural Calendar
Soil temperatures have often fallen into the 30s throughout the Lower Midwest by this point in the year. The Christmas tree harvest is almost over. Odds against the survival of garden vegetables rise sharply as the full force of the December 15th cold front settles in.

Daybook
1982: Chard has finally been killed by the cold, kale eaten by rabbits. Parsley and chives are still all right, purple deadnettle and mint unharmed.

1983: Carrots pulled from the garden, firm, medium sized, some of the most consistent I've grown.

1997: The second day in a row of sun and temperatures in the 50s. Wispy, morning cirrus clouds streaked the sky, made me feel there was more warmth to come. I drove to Fairborn; there was something about the city streets, something in the color, the way the sun lay across the lawns, that reminded me of spring in Minneapolis. On the way home, I saw a large hawk above Dayton-Yellow Springs Road. At dusk, the sky was rose color and with the windswept high clouds that had adorned the morning and afternoon. Just before dark, two flocks of starlings circled the shopping center where I had stopped; they swooped and dove and climbed, intersecting and separating before they finally settled for the night. On the way home, I saw the moon rising yellow in the cirrus over Dayton Street, bigger than I'd ever seen it before.

2000: In spite of one of the coldest Novembers and Decembers in recent history, the pear leaves still hold on in town, many still green.

2004: Euonymus leaves were darkened and hydrangea leaves curled by the cold of the last two nights. A few euonymus berries hang on by the back box elder.

2005: At 5:50 this evening, the sky clear, the temperature about 20 degrees, a screech owl called steadily from the back trees.

2008: Crows at 7:50 this morning. Inventory in the alley and the yard: grasses pale and bent, hulls peeling and unraveling on the black walnuts, some Osage fruits nibbled by squirrels or raccoons, hoary goldenrod and great ragweed broken, blackened euonymus drooping, chicory twisted, burdock leaves collapsed and brown, sweet rocket, pokeweed hollow and empty, garlic mustard, tall ragwort, celandine, poppies, thistles still green but limp and frozen, empty small white and New England asters, limp *stella d'oro* foliage, brittle lily stalks, chives flat and pale, only a few parsley stalks still standing.

2010: Crows were the only birds accompanying me when I walked Bella this morning. A dozen, maybe more, black buzzards by the side of the road on the way to Springfield. And great murders of crows were flying back and forth across the highway.

2011: Crows at 7:35 this morning, partly cloudy, rosy cirrus, 28 degrees.

2012: Another very soft morning, close to 60 by noon. Crows late at 7:50, two cardinals singing strong when I went out at 9:20, robins peeping and a medium-sized flock of starlings whistling.

2014: The last mild day before a cold front moves in, the four koi swimming all around the pond. In the garden, almost every day lily clump has melted like the hostas, and it is hard to tell the grasses from the lily foliage. And all the brown autumn stems of false boneset, New England asters, and phlox are bent with age and weather, breaking down.

2015: Inventory in the yard in this mild December (possibly the warmest in history): More hellebore buds; spreading chickweed, grasses, ground ivy, mint and henbit; wild onions up to a foot tall; snowdrop spears up an inch under the mulch; a few crocus leaves have come up; motherwort leaves in clumps; more waterleaf appearing; new sprouts of lamium, and many lamium plants in bloom; algae clouding and greening the pond water more; large and small koi feeding; robins in the yard, calling. From New Orleans, Jill sends photographs of numerous tropical vines with flowers, a rose bush with pink blossoms, a purple azalea in full bloom, and an aged goldenrod – still mostly gold – the last piece of autumn reaching to the Gulf.

2016: A second night of temperatures below 12 degrees, the land snow covered throughout the area.

2019: Meghan Bachman writes: "Not in YS, but close! I saw two bald eagles perched atop dead trees overlooking the Little Miami River a few miles south on US-68, just north of the 235 intersection, across the street from the barn with the 4-H quilt."
This is the fourth sighting so far this year. I recorded four in 2018, one in 2017, one in 2016. Is the history of the local bald eagle writing itself with these sightings? Have eagles been

here for years and no one talked about it? Whatever the case, these past two years are a kind of preliminary base line, which will hopefully be expanded.

2020: A long murder of crows crossed above me as I walked Ranger this morning at sunrise. Major snowstorm threatens the East Coast. Light snow here. The entire period between the 12th and today bookends perigee and the new moon with cold and precipitation from the Midwest to the Atlantic.

Journal

At the end of July, I planted winter tomatoes for the greenhouse. I put in a package of the imported Shirleys (thirteen seeds - fifty cents a seed), a dozen Big Boys, and a half a dozen Gardener's Delights, a small early variety.

My greenhouse lies behind a south wall, twelve feet of glass tall, twenty-eight feet wide. When clouds permit, the sun shines on most of the plants from the middle of the morning until three or so in the afternoon, even on the shortest days of the year.

Tomatoes are tolerant of low winter light. Given a good start outside in the summer, they begin to climb by the beginning of October. They are over my head by the middle of November, reaching up to the top of the first tier of windows, shutting out the bare branches of the hedge outside, and the neighbor's house. I let their suckers go where they choose.

By December, the plants have risen to ten feet, and when I sit in the wicker chair beneath them, they shade me from the noon, and they dapple the moonlight on the brick wall behind me.

At twelve feet, their peak in January, they are peerless allies, angels whose green wings protect me from the winter. Grown flat up against the glass, they are a living barrier, an insulation of spirit, as well as a gauge of a certain balance I keep with the outside. Neither the tomatoes nor I were meant to last beyond a predetermined threshold. Our alliance is a fantasy that will blacken and wilt if something goes awry, or if just one stone breaks through our glass.

Now late at night, in the center of a storm, I sit in the thrill of that dark and peril, and I listen to the wind, and I wonder at the strength and fragility of the tomatoes. While the snow builds up on the windows, I wonder at our ingenuity, our ephemeral beauty and

96

our reckless defiance.

A winter season
of the land or of the heart
strips us of all that can fall away
and leaves us what endures.

Margaret Lacy

December 17th
The 351st Day of the Year

The Sunne is spent, and now his flasks
Send forth light squibs, no constant rayes;
The world's whole sap is sunke:
The world's whole sap is sunke.

John Donne

Sunrise/set: 7:51/5:12
Day's Length: 9 hours 21 minutes
Average High/Low: 39/24
Average Temperature: 32
Record High: 66 – 1984
Record Low: - 10 – 1989

The Daily Weather
The 17th brings a warm afternoon above 50 degrees just five percent of the years. It offers highs in the 40s on 35 percent of the years, 30s on 25 percent, 20s on 25 percent, teens on five percent, and single digits on five percent. The sun shows through more than half the days, but chances of rain or snow are 50 to 60 percent, with a thunderstorm one year in a quarter of a century. Eighty-five percent of all the nights dip below 32 degrees. One dawn in 20 falls below zero.

The Natural Calendar
Milder weather as far north as Chicago may open pussy willows and draw up snowdrops, crocus and aconites in benign Decembers, but along the Gulf of Mexico, warm winds are already shortening the dormancy of trees and shrubs, hurrying the gestation of spring. Across coastal Georgia, sweet gums and yellow poplars finally lose their leaves, and their buds swell almost immediately to replace the loss. In central Florida, red maples open, and Jessamine produces its yellow blossoms.

Daybook
1986: A cardinal sang at 9:30 this morning, and sparrows were loud

and shrill all afternoon.

1988: Crows and starlings in the yard this morning and along the east fencerow. Sparrows chirp all day in the bare forsythia hedge.

1992: At National Road and U.S. 68, hundreds of crows in the west wood lot. Tonight, Barb told me about finding trees felled by beavers on the west side of the Jacoby area.

1994: Coming back from walking the dog about nine o'clock this evening, I found a woolly-bear caterpillar crawling slowly by the front door. I wondered if I ought to bring it in, let it make its cocoon in the warm greenhouse; but then, I thought, it might emerge early, might come out in February and flutter around the plants, dying before early spring. So I picked it up and put it under the leaves in the raspberry bed. The rest of December is supposed to be mild; maybe it will survive.

1997: Another night of the moon's third quarter, the land bright with lunar light when I got up at 5:00. Dawn was soft and orange. No sparrows singing along Xenia Avenue. No crows heard, no cardinals.

1999: On the way to Springfield: Flocks and flocks of crows and starlings, the world full of birds. The same a few days ago when I came this way. At campus, a chorus of sparrows in the crab apples. The sky is streaked with cirrus, windswept.

2004: A little after midnight, a skunk sprayed under the house, and we spent the night in the spare bedroom, the attic fan running, pumping out the odor. A cardinal sang once just as the orange sun was coming up from the southeast. As Mike and I walked along the river, a small flock of turkey vultures circled overhead. Toward town, crows were calling. Along the woods floor, the euonymus was dark and curled from the cold. The vines that had climbed through the trees showed only their white seed casings; their last fallen red berries lay along the paths. Bella did not pick up any burs on the walk – that's been the case for a month of walks now.

2005: Drove to Springfield late this afternoon. Three long formations of geese were flying south along the highway, hundreds of birds. And near the mall, the giant flock of winter crows was back after seeming to stay away for years. In the front yard, honeysuckle berries hold to their branches. Downtown, many pear leaves hold, burned from the cold December.

2006: Temperatures have been way above normal since we returned from Florida last week. Robins were peeping in the yard when I went outside this morning. Cardinals were singing off and on. When I walked Bella at about 9:00, I heard a dove calling over toward Stafford Street.

2008: The first dirty orange Osage fruits seen today, right next to several that had been eaten by squirrels. No birds heard on my walk through the alley this morning. Ice on the sidewalks and streets here; Jeni expects more snow in Portland.

2009: Crows at 7:39 this morning. Jeanie saw two buzzards in the roost when she walked with Chris around 8:00. And Casey called at 11:20: Two flocks of sandhill cranes over the Bryan Center and Xenia Avenue. I went out on my front porch and could hear them half a mile away on High Street.

2010: As I drove through Goes Station this noon, a vast cloud of starlings and blackbirds was hovering and then swooping above the road. On the way to Alpha, crows were feeding in a cornfield and more starlings were out looking for food. Abroad: Neysa reports snow in Capri, Italy and in Sardinia. Her pipes froze in Spoleto, and northern Europe is in deep freeze. Here in the United States, a great rainstorm is moving in against California, Oregon and Washington.

2011: The red-bellied woodpecker came by the first time in months, and jays, cardinals, chickadees and sparrows fed heavily until the big Cooper's hawk flew in and sat on top of the tallest bird feeders. (On December 11, 2017, a Red-tailed Hawk came hunting on the bird feeder, too. Or maybe I have misidentified one or the other.)

2012: After a very mild autumn, several daffodils are five inches high, buds straining. Snowdrops have been about an inch out of the ground for weeks. About a third of the pussy willows have pushed out a ways. In the middle of the afternoon, the first thunderstorm in over a month brought hard rain, frightened Bella and Monk, the cat.

2013: Snow still covers the ground from over a week ago, but a deep thaw is forecast for the 20th. A robin was peeping in the honeysuckles a little after 8:00 when I went out with the dogs. When I was downtown, I started talking to Rebecca about people we missed at this time of year, and then when I looked up, I saw a "V" formation of sandhill cranes flying southwest across Xenia Avenue. The time was 4:05. Tonight on the news, the anchor reported that this past November had been the warmest on record for the world.

2016: At 7:25 in the evening after an all-day rain and thaw, John Whitmore called and left a message: "I just stepped out onto my porch, like about three minutes ago, and I could hear that sandhill cranes were flying over. I could hear them calling as they came over the hilltop near my house. And then I went inside to get your number, and I heard them again, It's amazing - I can't believe it. I wasn't spending the evening outside, and I just went out and there they were in the dark!" Carolyn Mullen, who lives a mile or so north of John, also reported seeing sandhill cranes near this date, probably one of the flocks John sighted. SEP

2017: Mild in the 40s, rain approaching from the southwest. Crows at 7:30 this morning, and robins peeping all around the yard, sparrows and starlings chattering. I went out into the back yard for the first time in several days, and I found that all the Osage leaves had finally come down, and I missed their collapse! And downtown, the pear leaves had all fallen, too.

2020: Kay sent a photo of a violet in bloom at Clifton Gorge.

.

Late lies the wintry Sun a-bed,
A frosty, fiery sleepy-head;
Blinks but an hour or two; and then,
A blood-red orange, sets again.

Robert Louis Stevenson

December 18th
The 352nd Day of the Year

In the least
As well as in the greatest of His works
Is ever manifest His presence kind;
As well in swarms of glittering insects, seen
Quick to and from within a foot of air,
Dancing a merry hour, then seen no more,
As in the systems of resplendent worlds,
Through time revolving in unbound space.

Carlos Wilcox

Sunrise/set: 7:51/5:12
Day's Length: 9 hours 21 minutes
Average High/Low: 38/24
Average Temperature: 32
Record High: 62 – 1967
Record Low: - 8 – 1884

The Daily Weather
There is a 15 percent chance of highs in the 50s today (only one percent for 60s), thirty percent for 40s, fifteen percent for 30s, twenty-five percent for 20s, fifteen percent for deep cold in the teens or colder. Below-zero mornings occur ten to 15 percent of the time, making this the day most likely to have such conditions so far this winter. The sun appears on only 30 percent of December 18ths. Rain falls 20 percent of the time, snow 25 percent.

The Natural Calendar
Sol Invictus: From Yin to Yang
On December 1st, the sun reached its earliest setting (5:10 p.m.) in Yellow Springs, and it continues to set at that time until the Season of Later Sunsets starts on December 14th, when the sun goes down at 5:11 p.m. instead of 5:10. Sunset continues to move later in the day throughout the next six months, gaining 9 minutes in December, 32 in January, 32 in February, 31 in March, 29 in April,

28 in May, and 11 in June. On July 2, this season ends and the Season of Earlier Sunsets begins.

The small advance in sunset time on December 14th, however, is offset by the sun continuing to rise later in the morning. And the point-counterpoint of time lost and gained creates a weeklong standoff between December 19th and December 25th during which our day's length remains its shortest of the year, 9 hours and 20 minutes. Solar declination reaches -23 degrees, 26 minutes, the great yin, the lowest point of the year's solar tide, on December 21st. It remains at that position on the 22nd, 23rd and 24th.

Then, on the 25th, the *sol invictus,* the "unconquered sun" celebrated by ancient Romans, makes the very first move towards spring, its declination shifting just a fraction of a degree from -23 minutes, 26 seconds to -23 minutes, 25 seconds. The following day, December 26, the later sunsets finally start to outstrip the stagnating later sunrises, and the day's length in Yellow Springs increases for the first time since the end of June.

Sunrise, however, keeps taking place slightly later up until New Year's Day, which begins of a ten-day period during which the sunrise occurs at 7:57 a.m. Throughout that time, the sun goes down a minute or two later each day, and by the time sunrise finally comes up a minute earlier on January 11, the day is 14 minutes longer than it was on Christmas, and the reversal of the annual yin tide and the turn toward the warm yang of summer are complete.

The Shooting Stars

The Ursid Meteors arrive this week; they are visible near the Big and Little Dippers, the "Ursid" or "bear" constellations, through Christmas, usually peaking on December 21-22.

Daybook

1983: I dug carrots and beets from the frozen ground this afternoon. Most were damaged or spoiled from the hard freeze of the past week.

1987: Nice size chubs caught in the pool just below Grinnell Mill dam.

1989: Three nights in a row below zero, and a week of very cold weather have iced the river, leaving just a few patches open. Four inches of snow on the ground, the Japanese honeysuckle blackening as the temperature remains below 20 for days on end.

1992: North along Upper Valley Pike, a soybean field full of crows, maybe a thousand. At home, the finch feeder is consistently full of finches, maybe a fourth of them house finches. Starlings have taken over the suet cage.

1994: In the warm November and December, daffodils have begun to come up along the front sidewalk. Some snow crocus foliage has emerged completely; the plants might even bloom if there is a warm spell soon.

1997: I went west down Jacoby Road to the old bridge foundation, then followed the streambed toward the swamp. Even though the temperature was only in the low 40s and frost still covered the swamp grass, a moth was out fluttering through the trees. Along the forest floor, chickweed was strong, leaves small but thriving in this mild winter. Moss was starting to grow on a few rotting logs.

Standing by the head of the swamp, I listened to the brook that drained it, the water barely audible, a rustle, shuffle. Up the path a ways, the first spring came through the hillside surrounded by dark green ragwort; it was a little louder than the brook, its rhythm steady, hollow, with recurring beats.

The next spring, produced a steady, high song through stones, punctuated with plunks. The third spring was mute, stopped by ice and leaves. The fourth spring, the one by the old the springhouse with its broken roof tiles and earth-brown blocks: a soft trickle through the rocks and cress and pool, uneven syncopated ringing.

In the distance, a jet plane and a flock of crows. Then a chickadee in the honeysuckle ahead. Then a train off in Fairborn blowing its urban horn, sounding lonely even here in the sun.

The fifth spring, bubbling out of a cliff that drops from the west side of the path, made a more liquid, fatter sound as it fell maybe ten feet to the rocks and cement and moss and cress of the old man-made pool below. A sound like rain in the eaves.

The sixth spring, the intermittent spring in the small canyon just before I reached the river dam, was dry. The rock formation suggests this must have been a waterfall of icemelt ten or fifteen millennia ago. Against the silence of this relic, I turned west into the heavy, symphonic sound of the Little Miami River.

1998: The body of a carpenter bee lay frozen on the back porch this morning. He had been tricked, pulled out of his winter nest by yesterday's warm weather, and then caught in last night's cold.

2004: Yesterday's skunk spraying continues to make the house stink!

2005: At 1:30 this morning, a tremendous scratching at the south eaves: some kind of animal broke in, walked around in the attic a while. Then I drifted off to sleep.

2007: Cold this morning in the low 20s, about two inches of snow remaining on the ground. Crows came by at about 7:30, then moved on. The birds are active at the feeders, a few starlings on a Stafford Street black walnut tree, but it is a quiet, frozen day, the sky pale gold, hazy, the sun barely visible through the trees. The sun went down last night behind the shed, the far southwest corner of its winter trajectory.

2008: Crows late this morning: 8:15. A cardinal heard in the distance near Phillips Street when I walked the alley with Bella close to 10:00.

2009: The buzzards are still here, according to Jeanie and Chris; they saw a large flock of them this morning at the Corey Street roost. And Jenny Copperwaite wrote this afternoon about seeing sandhill cranes: "Hi Bill! I saw them! For the very first time in my life here in YSO I saw them! Actually I HEARD them first. I've never heard anything like it before – it was AMAZING. What kind of cranes are they and where plus how far are they going?"

2011: First crows at 7:50 this morning.

2012: First crows at 7:50 today. Casey called at 9:15 to tell me he'd seen a flock of maybe a dozen black buzzards down on Grinnell Road at a deer carcass below the water treatment plant.

2013: Walking Bella at around 8:30 this morning, sun about four fingers up over the southeast, I heard a blue jay and a tufted titmouse,

106

then came across a small flock of starlings feeding near Lawson Place. When I took the garbage out near 10:00, a cardinal was singing and singing. While I was at work, Kathryn Hitchcock left a message that as she was driving from Kettering about 10:30, she saw a large "V" of sandhill cranes. She said she could see the morning sun shining on their bellies.

2016: Cloudy and raw, light snow, icy highways: John Blakelock called (10:40 a.m.): "I heard the sandhill cranes when I was in the house and then went out, saw seven of them, and then a straggler came in pretty low. I thought I had missed them this year, but then there they were!"

Less than hour later, Tim Barhorst wrote: "Saw around 40-50 sandhills flying south over the North Glen and headed toward the south Glen. They were quite noisy and clearly heated even though they were flying pretty high up in a couple of "V" formations."

2017: Once again, a mild day in the 40s with the December 20 cold front dissolving (in spite of new moon today) in apogee.

2018: Mild and clear today, near 40 degrees. John Blakelock reported a surge in geese activity in the area, gathering and calling, one flock rising into a long "V" and heading south. After weeks carrying large buds, the one of the large Christmas cacti finally has one blossom.

2019: High clouds throughout the day, chilling north wind. Anne Randolph called at 9:50 this morning to report a flock of 15 sandhill cranes overhead, and then Betty Ross called at 4:15, saying she saw one flock of 32 and then another flock of 36, heading south above the Arboretum Trail in John Bryan Park, and then the two flocks came back over where she was and began circling, most likely waiting for more cranes to come. Tonight, the wind is still, Orion visible through haze in the east, cold deepening.

Journal

Several years ago, I took our two bulldogs out for a walk in the woods. It had snowed a few more inches over night, for a total of several feet in some places, and we were the first to navigate the path.

The dogs worked their way through the high snow, the puppy, six months old, breaking trail with his chest. The older bulldog was invigorated by the cold, ranged on ahead, leaping fallen trees, racing back from time to time for reassurance and to check the puppy.

Above the dam, the river was frozen over. Below, in the open channel that led to the mill, the water was black and the current strong and loud. Halfway to the old sycamore where vultures used to roost, a formation of geese flew over heading north.

Then at the bend of he river, suddenly there was a whinny of robins as we walked into a large flock that had been here feeding on honeysuckle berries since October. On both sides of the path, birds moed through the undergrowth, calling and playing. I felt surround by and included in several separate societies then; I was part of the flocks and part of the pack.

Making my way through the snow, I thought back about the year I used to take a litter of puppies out through the overgrown fields of a farm I rented. On those walks, I experienced an excitement forgotten until today's outing in the snow, and I recognize now how important that excitement was and how I miss it.

I think that when I am lonely, it is because I've slipped too far away from some prerequisite communion, a hard running with the pack, a romp with my clan. I think we were all made to dance and cavort together in community of species.

Although the lesson for me has much to do with my relationships with people (or the lack of relationships), I do not seem to learn that that lesson from or with other people. I only glimpse its truth in these woods with the dogs and with the robins, recalling our ancestry and our innate design, what we must have been and still could be.

So short a day, and life so quickly hasting.

Carmina Burana

December 19th
The 353rd Day of the Year

When earth is newly clad in snow
And wonder's dusted off the mantel of the commonplace
And left it round and soft,
When earth and sky both share a glow
When all is light aloft, alow,
My heart just wants to romp and laugh
When all the world's become one path.
No need to probe with crook or staff
When all the world's become one path.

Robert Paschell

Sunrise/set: 7:52/5:12
Day's Length: 9 hours 20 minutes
Average High/Low: 38/23
Average Temperature: 31
Record High: 60 – 1895
Record Low: - 16 – 1884

The Daily Weather

December 19th brings completely overcast conditions two years out of three, and this date has a 50 percent chance of precipitation, with the odds weighted a bit more towards rain than snow. Today's distribution of high temperatures: teens or 20s come 30 percent of the time; 30s come 30 percent and 40s another 30 percent, 50s only ten percent. Below-zero mornings occur 15 percent of the time, and morning lows above freezing are equally infrequent.

The Natural Calendar

Greenhouse workers are taking cuttings from mother plants for future stocks of varieties such as impatiens and geraniums. Preparations are also underway for the seeding of the earliest bedding plants. Between the 19th and the 25th, the day's length remains steady at nine hours 20 minutes in Yellow Springs, the shortest span of the year.

1986: Geese continue to fly over town, have let up only a little since middle fall.

1988: South Glen: Southwest wind loud and warm, geese flying back and forth, cumulus tousled, white and gray, low and fast, sparrows swarming in the aster seeds; then I almost stumbled over two people, naked, making love in the dead goldenrod. I saw clothes, coats, thrown across the grass, knees akimbo. The couple paid me no attention, and I turned quickly away, walked on, somehow renewed, more optimistic than I had been before, with a sense that the world was doing what it should.

1989: Goldenrod seeds about three-fourths gone.

1990: The sparrows are quiet, waiting as I come to take the bird feeder inside to fill. When I go back out and hang it in the tree, the cry goes up, wild chirping.

1992: The crows were still flying east or northeast along the freeway today. This flock must have reached at least three or four miles.

1997: Only a few sparrows chirping in the pear trees on Xenia Avenue this morning. Delicate new blue growth noticed on the junipers by the pond; it must have started in October or November. Beside the junipers, a couple of pale blue pansies are still in bloom.

1999: The koi have finally settled in for winter now, passive as I clean out the pump, unafraid in the slow peace of hibernation. Today I went to mass for the first time in a year, the season, the short days, finally getting to me.

2001: This morning as I was working outside fixing the kitchen table in the sun, a black housefly came and lit on the wood beside me.

2004: Looking back over the daybook journal, I wonder what happened to the couple I discovered making love in the field at South Glen back on this day in 1988. Do they remember the day like I do? Is their ritual as durable as mine? December voyeur, I want everything I observe to hold some kind of significance. In Chaos Theory, the infinite number of unknown factors and forces short-circuits the possibility of accurate prediction or perfect understanding. Able to experience only a tiny fraction of the world, I take refuge in conjecture. But that way, I assume that what I see is deficient, insufficient. What if everything is what it seems to be? Weighing each event and object equally, I might see the universe without discrimination or hierarchies of value. Nature no longer remains a mystery that way, its motions no longer separate from human motions. Meaning is simple. What you see is what you get.

2008: The second December cardinal call heard this morning about 11:00. From the Plains to Boston, heavy snow and winds. Tat had another snow day. Only rain in Yellow Springs, and a few hours of sun, highs in the 50s.

2009: The first snow of the year covered all the branches this morning, showing off the daffodil spears that had grown up in the warm November. A screech owl was calling softly at 7:00. A small flock of cowbirds joined the sparrows and songbirds at the feeders today. The first finch in weeks showed up at the finch seed. On the news tonight, details about a huge storm that has buried the East and is moving toward the Northeast. Record snowfalls in Washington, D.C.

2010: The first striped-breasted sparrow seen at the front feeder about 11:00. Just before 1:00 this afternoon, the back trees filled with thousands of starlings. Among their calls and whistles, I heard peeping robins. The giant flock remained in the neighborhood through the afternoon, circling and gathering, clucking and whistling and cackling, and I took Bella down toward the park where some of the cottonwood trees across the street were black with birds.

When I walked through the crab apple trees, a small number of robins flew off toward the starlings. And the gathering of birds seemed to have nothing to do with feeding, like the flocks I've seen in the fields, but rather some kind of reconnoitering or taking stock, a pause to scout or communicate, maybe an intermediate stop in migration. They were shy and restless as I approached their trees, so I ended up just standing still in the snow and watching them and listening to them.

2013: Again today, a cardinal sang well after sunup. Robins were whinnying, sparrows chattering. In the alley, pale orange hulls of bittersweet lay scattered in the melting snow.

2015: Delayed, perhaps, by a November almost ten degrees above normal and an equally warm December, the sandhill cranes finally passed over Yellow Springs. John Blakelock called as soon as he heard the first cries at about 4:00. Then Kurt Weigard called at 4:15, had sighted them when he was standing at the corner of Green and North West College Street.

Then Audrey Hackett wrote: "I heard and saw sandhill cranes this afternoon! I live on North High Street, and they were flying in the southern sky 20-25 minutes ago--about 4:15 p.m.? To see them, I had to look into the sun, so I only caught a glimpse of a dark and twisting strand of birds before being totally dazzled. But I could hear them for half a minute or more."

And when I saw Peter Hayes in the grocery store, he said that Mary Sue had seen a flock flying really high over Dayton-Yellow Springs Road not long after 4:00 p.m. When I went to see Lori for a haircut, she told me she had seen the cranes over Springfield that afternoon. And then Bob wrote to say he had seen them over southwest central Champaign County about the same time "circling higher and higher from a couple old gravel pit ponds, then working south."

So there were six reports that suggest that major waves of sandhills came over the region.

2016: To Jill's house: robins and starlings moving restlessly through the high trees, chortling and chirping.

2017: Raking leaves in the mild afternoon: robins peeping in the yards around me. In the greenhouse, all of the Christmas cacti hold their flowers, geraniums and begonias still in bloom, vincas slowly losing blossoms. At the feeders, finches have been a steady presence through this gentle Early Winter. In the south garden, about half of the black hosta seeds hold to their calices. Along the south border, the bamboo, some maybe twenty or thirty feet tall, keeps its deep green.

2018: Robins peeping along Stafford Street this morning.

2019: Mike from south of Xenia called this morning to say he had seen the sandhill cranes yesterday afternoon, probably the same ones that Betty saw, the flock augmented by then to near 100.

Chunky and noisy,
but with stars in their black feathers,
they spring from the telephone wire
and instantly
they are acrobats
in the freezing wind.

Mary Oliver, from "Starlings in Winter"

The dark
rooms hold our heads on pillows, waiting
day, through the snow falling and fallen
in the darkness between inconsecutive
dreams. The brain burrows in the earth
and sleeps, trusting dawn....

Wendell Berry

Sunrise/set 7:53/5:13
Day's Length: 9 hours 20 minutes
Average High/Low: 38/23
Average Temperature: 31
Record High: 63 – 1895
Record Low: - 12 – 1963

The Daily Weather

There is a 50 percent chance of clear or partly clear conditions today, but rain comes 25 percent of the time, snow 20 percent. This morning and the morning of the 26th are the most likely (about 20 percent likely) to record below-zero temperatures in all December. High temperatures are in the teens 20 percent of the time, in the 20s ten percent, in the 30s twenty percent, in the 40s thirty percent, and two out of every ten December 20ths provide a thaw in the 50s or 60s.

The Natural Calendar

In the dark afternoons in December, orchids are in their prime. Under lights, in a greenhouse, or in a south window, many varieties bloom before Christmas.

Daybook

1984: On a walk downtown, new iris foliage seen. They are pacing fresh candy-lily leaves by the front fence.

1987: Two-inch iris growth seen. A muskrat sighted above Grinnell Mill dam; the river is low and clear, even after two days of hard rain. Birds active and loud around the yard.

1989: A sundog in the west at 4:30 this afternoon. Long flock of crows seen heading east from Springfield. Do they follow the highway because the road follows some ancient natural flyway?

1994: Down the path from Grinnell swamp, moss has sent out its orange flower stems as though March were here.

1997: I watched the sun come over the east horizon at 8:14 this morning. The houses across the street hide it for 20 minutes after its official rising time on my charts.

1998: Mother-of-millions is budding in the greenhouse. Outside in the pond, algae grows thick in the shallow end, and the waterfall slows to a trickle, the pump filling with late-autumn sludge.

1999: Rain in the dark morning, autumn drought ending, the rivers finally filling below Grinnell Bridge.

2004: The skunk odor in the house from the 17th has finally subsided. Overnight, a deep cold wave came through, pushing temperatures down to near zero. The pond pump stopped, and the water froze over. I had to go out and break the ice with a hammer, and then I plugged in the pond heater.

 2008: Jeni calls from Portland: Ten inches of snow forecast for tonight. And that after a week of snow and ice when schools were closed three of five days.

2009: A pileated woodpecker flew off from the back woodlot when I came out to get wood after church this noon.

2010: The ground has been snow-covered since the beginning of the month, and more snow is forecast for tonight. The starlings were still in the back trees and around the park when I went out with Bella at about 8:45 this morning. As I turned up Dayton Street, a swooping flock hovered and turned and then settled near the cottonwood trees. When I reached the crab apple trees, I could see smaller numbers of birds in various trees, but not the immense flocks like yesterday.

2013: Almost all the snow melted in a thaw that has brought temperatures into the 50s today. This evening, light rain.

2015: In spite of highs only in the 30s, the first pale green hellebore flower opened in the dooryard today. The koi in the pond did not react when I threw a little food into the pond, the water temperature in the 40s chilling the fish but also contributing to the clearest water all year.

2017: Last leaves of the Osage raked. Jill and I saw two large murmurations of starlings coming back from Beavercreek. Robins still peeping in the yard. At Ellis Pond at sunset, the water still and orange, the air clear, windless, black trees sharp against the sky, some fragile ice at the south end of the pond. A fat raccoon caught in the attic this evening, after more than a week of trying to catch him.

2019: Mike reports bald eagles nesting south of Spring Valley.

Long is our winter,
Dark is our night.
Expectant are our hearts.
Come, O Radiant, Healing, Loving Light

From a 15th Century German Hymn

December 21st
The 355th Day of the Year

Under the snow,
just after solstice:
all of the fire of May
has been hidden, but
a thousand miles south,
in ambivalent borderlands,
cold starts to flicker and loses momentum:
winter and summer a fulcrum
as thin as a bud or an hour.
And somewhere between
the marshes of Glynn
on the south coast of Georgia
and Everglades swamps,
somewhere between them
at peak of the tide,
the poles are reversing:
Instead of receding,
the summer is swelling,
and stirring the coals
far, far within,
of the distant, impossible
core of the spring.

bf

Sunrise/set: 7:53/5:13
Day's Length: 9 hours 20 minutes
Average High/Low: 38/23
Average Temperature: 30
Record High: 65 – 1967
Record Low: - 15 – 1989

The Daily Weather

Skies are overcast five years in ten. Snow falls one year in five, rain one year in four. Highs in 60s occur five percent of the time,

50s twenty percent, 40s five percent. Chilly days in the 30s come 55 percent of the time, and there is a five percent chance each of highs only in the 20s, teens, and single-digits. Lows drop below freezing three-fourths of the nights, but below-zero temperatures come only once or twice in a decade on this date.

The Weather in the Week Ahead

Two major cold waves ordinarily dominate this time of the year. The first front comes in on the 21st or 22nd, and the second arrives between the 23rd and the 26th. Christmas Day is typically the brightest day of the week, bringing a 70 percent chance of sun. The 28th is the darkest day, with a 70 percent chance of clouds. Snow falls half the time on Christmas Eve and on the two days before New Year's Day. The 26th is typically the coldest day of the week and has almost a 40 percent chance of highs just in the teens or 20s.

Natural Calendar:
An Approximate Schedule of Cardinal Song
from Winter Solstice to Summer Solstice
in Yellow Springs
Latitude 39 degrees, 48 minutes N
Longitude -83 degrees 53 minutes W

During the time of winter solstice, early mornings are quiet in Yellow Springs. The cardinals sleep late, singing only sporadically after about 7:40 a.m. By the middle of January, however, the steady growth of the day's length intensifies the mating cycle, and cardinal song begins to consistently precede sunrise by about half an hour through equinox. When April approaches, the birds rise even earlier, sometimes calling an hour before dawn. By the end of the end of May, most cardinals reach their limit around 4:00 a.m. After that, they settle into the longest days of the year, sleeping a little later in the mornings, their music softening as the nights grow longer.

The following schedule, based on observations in Yellow Springs over several decades, sketches the approximate parallel of cardinal song to sunrise. Although sunrise times are different everywhere, the approximate interval between dawn and cardinal song is relatively stable. Temperature, cloud cover, precipitation and, most likely, individual birds all significantly influence the song times, sometimes changing them by 15 or 20 minutes. Still, the overall pattern is somewhat predictable, and it provides one more context for natural history as well as for spiritual geography (both of which Kathleen Norris ties to conversion).

Day	Sunrise	First Cardinal Song
December 21	7:53 a.m.	7:40 a.m.
January 1	7:57 a.m.	7:40 a.m.
January 10	7:57 a.m.	7:30 a.m.
January 26	7:49 a.m.	7:22 a.m.
January 31	7:45 a.m.	7:20 a.m.
February 3	7:42 a.m.	7:15 a.m.
February 5	7:40 a.m.	7:10 a.m.
February 9	7:36 a.m.	7:04 a.m.
February 16	7:27 a.m.	6:57 a.m.
February 20	7:22 a.m.	6:45 a.m.
March 3	7:06 a.m.	6:33 a.m.
March 9	6:57 a.m.	6:30 a.m.
March 13	6:50 a.m.	6:16 a.m.
March 20	6:39 a.m.	6:10 a.m.
March 24	6:33 a.m.	6:02 a.m.
March 27	6:28 a.m.	5:55 a.m.
March 31	6:21 a.m.	5:44 a.m.
April 2	6:18 a.m.	5:34 a.m.
April 16	5:56 a.m.	5:12 a.m.
April 21	5:49 a.m.	5:05 a.m.
May 2	5:34 a.m.	4:43 a.m.
May 19	5:17 a.m.	4:07 a.m.
May 23	5:14 a.m.	4:04 a.m.
June 21	5:06 a.m.	4:04 a.m.

All times are given in Eastern Standard Time.

Daybook

1983: Jacoby: I walked the whole swamp easily today because of the ice. Everything was frozen over except the stream channels. Skunk cabbage was up three or four inches in some places, blackened from the cold. Dock, leafcup, buttercup, mint, ragwort and henbit foliage was burned and prostrate from the week- long cold wave, but water cress was bright and green, frozen in the ice. On the high ground, one fern, apparently unhurt by the weather, was sticking out from under a snow-covered log.

1990: In the warmth and rain, a rose has formed a large, red bud above the brittle mums by Neysa's west window.

1993: The witch hazel on Dayton Street has kept its color through the month. I wonder if it's really still blooming, or if the golden petals are petrified in the cold and will hang on dead until spring.

1999: First real cold weather of the winter, temperatures only rising do the middle 20s; single digits tonight. I put the heater into the pond, the west end of the water all iced over. Crows and seagulls brought the landscape alive as I drove north to Springfield. The ground was hard, bumpy with the frozen mole hills and grass clumps when I went out to get wood tonight.

2000: Last of the maple leaves are finally down.

2004: At dawn on this solstice, I watched from our bedroom window as the sun came up in the southeast from the crook of the Danielson's maple tree over the edge of Mrs. Timberlake's house. The skunk-catching man showed up at 11:00 a.m., set traps to capture the animals that have been causing problems under the house. "They'll be out tonight," he said. "There's a front coming in, and they'll be scavenging."

2008: Cold, windswept sky, ragged cumulus blown from the northwest, sun appearing and disappearing. One robin sitting on the east maple at the entry of the alley to Dayton Street. On the bark below it, a downy woodpecker looking for food. Across the northern tier of states, snow and storms from west to east. Here, nothing at all but highs in the teens. Tat says it is fifteen below zero there in Madison.

2009: As I was getting ready to send my column to the *News*, I received this e-mail from John Blakelock:
"I first saw the cranes on December 9, 2007. I was working for Chris Moore, putting a brick facing on a chimney at the

Thistle Creek development.   I always hear the cranes before I see them, and something mystical intoxicates me...it's like slipping into the dream state...a heightened consciousness.   Their call sounds like a downward glissando on a wooden xylophone.   They chatter so, gossiping amongst themselves about the silly humans below.   I was like, 'Oh my God, those are CRANESSSSS!'   We only saw about a dozen that day.   Chris told me he was out there on the weekend, tooling the joints, and saw hundreds: "They came and circled, and then more groups kept joining them," he said, "and finally, when they were all together, they headed off again south."

"This year I saw 18 on December 10… in Huber Heights…. I saw a lot more on the 13th.   I was working on my own house, up on scaffolding again (The cranes are so celestial, is there something about being up in the air that gives one closer access?). I was looking up at these wonderful wispy clouds: they looked as if they had been dragged and smeared by the jet stream.   I was thinking I should take some pictures of them to send to the Weather Channel.

"And then there was that weird sound, and my initial reaction is always disbelief, and then they appeared past the overhang of my roof. I called my mom because she is dying to see them. She could hear them. There were scores of them! The path they followed was like an amateur drawing on an Etch-a-sketch: south, then west, then south again. 'They're headed towards the high school!' I shouted into my cell phone.   She said she could hear them. I ran inside and grabbed the AA batteries out of the charger and loaded them into my camera and grabbed my keys and jumped into the car, flew down Dayton Street, took a left on East Enon, turned right on Hyde. Coming out of the huge dip at Jacoby Valley, I got a glimpse of the flock. 'There they are!' I shouted, 'I can see them!' I took a left on the road that runs past the vocational school, just past that church, briefly was on Route 235, then Routsong, finally saw them again as I approached Linebaugh, took a left and after half a mile slammed on the brakes and turned into somebody's driveway, and I intercepted them.

"I saw them again on the 16th. Actually heard them, from inside my house, they were making such a racket! They were circling over Mills Lawn, about a hundred of them. I called my mom and grabbed my camera and jumped in the car bet lost them on Dayton Street. They just vanished.

"I will never get jaded about seeing cranes, it's like seeing

123

angels. I get ecstatic about them."

2010: Cardinals came to the bird feeder in dark this morning at 7:41. Crows called eight minutes later. When I went outside for wood at 8:45, one of the back locust trees was filled with starlings.

2011: Three turkey vultures circling at the south edge of town.

2012: Juncos have been feeding here for the past three or four days, for the first time this winter.

2013: All the streams are flushed with snowmelt and rain, a high of 59 this afternoon. At Ellis, the pastures are partially flooded, the pond full. At the oak grove, the shingle oak, the sawtooth oak and the scarlet oak still hold their leaves, all brown.

2015: Wind and rain through the day as a warm front moves in before Christmas.

2017: After trapping a raccoon in the attic last night, I had hoped that there would be no more. But at five o'clock this morning: the loudest racket we had heard all autumn as several raccoons raced above us squealing and thumping.

2018: Mild, wet weather continues, the day in the 40s, barometer very low at 29.42.

2019: A mild, partly cloudy morning, robins peeping all around the Stafford Street alley, crows overhead, occasional cardinal song all near sunrise. Is this the outrider of Alabama winter? Leslie reports many juncos at her feeders daily.

O, Oriens,
Splendor lucis aeternae
Et sol justiciae:
Veni et illumina sedentes
In tenebris
Et umbra mortis.

O, new Dawn,
Shining with enduring Light,
Sun of Equilibrium:
Come and brighten us
Who wait in Darkness,
In the Shadow of Death.

"O" Antiphon for December 21
(8th Century A.D.)

See, Winter comes to rule the varied year....

James Thomson

Sunrise/set: 7:54/5:14
Day's Length: 9 hours 20 minutes
Average High/Low: 38/23
Average Temperature: 30
Record High: 62 – 1941
Record Low: - 20 – 1989

The Daily Weather

Highs are above 50 ten percent of the time today, and they reach into the 40s forty percent of the time. Thirties occur 30 percent of the afternoons; ten percent of the time, highs are only in the 20s; on ten percent of the days they do not get above ten degrees. Below-zero temperatures come only five percent of the mornings, but almost three-fourths of the days bring lows below 32 degrees. Chances of rain or snow remain steady at 45 percent.

The Natural Calendar

A tree, outbuilding, or neighbor's chimney is suitable for tracking solar movement as December comes to a close. The further north the sun progresses from the chosen landmark, the higher it will be at noon, the closer spring will be.

The deepest incursion of light through a south window at noon also provides a base line for measuring the receding winter. As the light retreats a little each day from its noon position at solstice, the south window becomes a gnomon that reveals the rising path of the sun.

Daybook

1986: The first mother-of-millions flowered in the greenhouse. Geese flew over at 5:20 p.m.

1988: Two robins seen in the yard this afternoon, and more heard in the neighborhood. Crows passed over from time to time. Sparrows waited in the poplar for me to come and feed them. Privets still hold their leaves on Dayton Street. First mother-of-millions flowered today.

1989: Record cold, 30 below on my thermometer (20 below in Dayton). Everything quiet until noon, then a wren came out to look for seeds along the south garden wall.

1992: Springfield: At first, I saw just a small group of crows in a soybean field not far from Springfield-Xenia Road. Then an hour later as I drove along Upper Valley Pike, I came onto a great murder of crows flying overhead, its source lost in the southwest, its destination stretching into the southeast. Tonight, Uncle Bill called from northern Minnesota: sunrise, he said, was 8:15, sunset 4:37, and the wind-chill was dropping toward 60 below. Tomorrow, he said, the days would begin to lengthen.

1998: Yesterday, a heavy all-day rain with highs in the 50s, and today the barometer is up to 30.60, temperatures not even making it out of the teens. At noon I went out to the car to go downtown, and on the driveway, still alive, an earthworm was trying to work its way to soft ground. I picked it up and tucked it under a stone where the ground did not seem frozen yet. At the mall, a robin was looking for red crab apples among the parking lot trees.

1999: The brightest full moon in 133 years, with perigee, cast clear, black shadows of the apple tree and the locust trees on the frozen lawn at five o'clock this morning.

2000: Walk to the Yellow Spring in the snow with Buttercup. Stillness and drifting flurries, large flakes, the landscape so changed by the winter that once I felt lost even though I was going down a path I had walked dozens of times before. I remembered the time I got lost hunting in my favorite woods in Wisconsin, how I panicked and started planning how I would spend the night. I was only a few yards from the road, but the snow was so heavy that my earlier tracks had filled up. The sky was so low and gray, visibility only a few yards, everything unfamiliar, every landmark covered up.

2003: Flocks of starlings have been performing graceful acrobatics all month. I took them for granted before. Now every time I drive somewhere, I see them playing in the sky.

2004: Twelve inches of snow today. The whole region has shut down.

2005: It struck me this morning that nature, without story, has no scaffold. Nor have I. Events and objects float in chaos until they are tied together with plot. I sometimes puzzle about enumeration: If is it the very stuff of description and setting, so then what? What happens? What does it mean? Or is the narrative about action and things all there is?

2007: Gerry and Carey visiting from Philadelphia: we all walked downtown in the mild, 55-degree afternoon. When they came by last year, the weather was the same.

2008: Bitter cold with sun, low of zero this morning. Sparrows and finches mob the feeders.

2011: Crows at 7:50 this morning. The downy woodpecker visited at 8:12, for the second time in as many days (after staying away for months). In the alley, a relatively large patch of deadnettle in bloom, pink flowers reach up to springtime height. All around me as I walked, the chirps and whistling of sparrows and starlings, and a turkey vulture flew by in the distance.

2012: To Gethsemani in Kentucky, the sky clearing up as I drove, cloudless along the Bluegrass Parkway, fields and pasture lands so green, glowing in the sun, four murmurations of starlings seen along the way.

2013: Just after midnight, I heard thunder, and then I woke up a little later to intense rainfall, almost like the sound of a train. At dawn, I saw the south yard was flooded. When I came back from church at noon, I noticed that the dooryard snowdrops had emerged overnight, were half an inch above the soil. Cardinals were singing off and on throughout the morning.

2015: I woke to rain, and then clearing skies by dawn, and the day warming into the 60s. Robins peeping around the neighborhood. Ed Oxley came by with pictures of his forsythia from December 15th and snowdrops that opened today. He said that he saw worms on the walk near his house; they had been driven out of the ground by the rain. Around the dooryard garden, more crocus and a few daffodil leaves are coming up. The hellebore garden near the Jeanie's redbud tree has nine fully open pale green blossoms. And Jill and I saw two yellow sulphur butterflies at the Glass Farm on our walk this afternoon.

2017: Very mild with very light rain, barometer dropping ahead of the Christmas cold front. The cranes knew the front was coming: Amy Crawford wrote: "My friend Lin and I were walking at the high school track this morning, and about 35 or 40 sandhill cranes flew over. It was about 8:40, Friday 12/22/17. What a delight! I also saw them a couple weeks ago over my home on Lamont Drive, also in the morning before 10 o'clock."

2018: Yucca seed heads losing their dark protective covering. At Ellis Pond just after sundown, west in the soybean field, over a hundred geese stood at attention in a row looking at me while I looked at them.

2019: Robins peeping all around the yard this morning as the Christmas cold front abdicates to days of sun and highs in the 40s and 50s. I often think that the overwintering robins are a recent phenomenon, but my notes reveal they have been here since I began to pay attention. On the sidewalk toward Limestone Street: bittersweet berries.

2020: John Blakelock called at 4:59 "You just missed cranes, a good sized "V" – probably 50 of them. I thought I was going to miss them this year.... Yay, yay!" And then a note from Liz Porter: "I just went outside (5:00 p.m.) with my compost, and I heard Sandhills to the south but did not see them. It sounded like a pretty big flock!"

Then a note from Megan: "I saw my first sandhill cranes

yesterday! What a strange and beautiful sound. A four-year-old said as they passed, 'They are singing to us.' At around 3 p.m., I saw a flock of around 25 flying southwest from Ellis Pond over Dayton Street near Winter St./Elm St. Then, at around 4:30 p.m., a second flock, this time of close to 50 flying southwest from Ellis Point over Dayton Street near High St/King St."

And then Audrey Hackett: Sandhill cranes to report! My husband and I saw, and heard, a flock of about 80 passing overhead as we were crossing the Mills Lawn green space at 5 p.m. They formed a sharp wedge, the lower line of which was much longer than the upper. The evening was cold and clear; the cranes were flying fairly high and calling distinctly; we longed to follow them."

Like the trees, we had to let each new year shape, tear and renew us until our unconscious habits fell like autumn leaves to the forest floor; and new, more conscious ways of doing things sprouted in their place.

Ken Carey

December 23rd
The 357th Day of the Year

Shine warmly down, thou Sun of noon-time,
On this chill pageant, melt and move
The winter's frozen heart with love.
And, soft and low, thou wind south-blowing,
Breathe through a veil of tenderest haze,
Thy prophecy of summer days.

John Greenleaf Whittier

Sunrise/set: 7:54/5:14
Day's Length: 9 hours 20 minutes
Average High/Low: 37/22
Average Temperature: 30
Record High: 59 – 1957
Record Low: - 8 – 1960

The Daily Weather

Highs in the 50s are more likely today than on most December days, such warmth occurring 20 percent of the years. Many afternoons, however, are chilly. There is a 25 percent chance of 40s, forty percent chance of 30s, fifteen percent chance of highs only in the 20s or teens. Chances of precipitation are 35 percent, a drop from yesterday's 45 percent. Completely overcast conditions darken the landscape five years in ten on this date.

Natural Calendar

Orchard grass, goldenrod, foxtail, Japanese knotweed, dock, virgin's bower, pepper grass, penny cress, garlic mustard, velvet leaf, mallow, Queen Anne's lace, parsnip, milkweed, water horehound, motherwort, bergamot, ironweed, jimson weed, mullein, yarrow, black-eyed Susan, burdock, cattail, dogbane, and teasel are some of the most common plants still available for dried winter bouquets.

Daybook

1982: Forget-me-not foliage is still strong, and a few chard plants are still alive, as are the purple deadnettle and chickweed, henbit, dandelion, parsley, chives, mallow, and garlic mustard.

1988: In the warm afternoon, cardinals sang off and on. Tips of crocus were coming up in front of the bookstore downtown. In the yard, multiflora rose buds looked ready to open. Standing against my back door, I watched the sun setting between the two Osage trees at the far corner of the yard, 240 degrees on my compass, exactly southwest. Geese flew over at 5:17 p.m.

1991: Some broccoli and Brussels sprouts still hold.

1993: Bitter cold moved in yesterday, but Diana reports hundreds of robins in the Antioch School trees. Are they the ones I've been seeing in the Glen - or a lost flock still moving south - or one disoriented, coming north two months early?

1999: The fallen leaves are coming apart now, letting go of their shapes, dissolving back into the ground. I can't tell a box elder from a maple or an Osage or mulberry leaf. The leaves accept the rain, their resilience turned to receptivity by the freezing and thawing. Their surfaces have become porous and absorbent, sometimes skeletal, letting all the weather through, offering no resistance. In the north garden, the ferns have fallen across the hostas, providing a mantle of protective mulch. Amaranth is bowing to set its seeds, the weakening of the stalk contributing to the planting. Black pokeberries dangle on their soft, dried stems. Foxtail grasses cling to one another, wave in the wind like lost caterpillars. Snapdragons finally succumb to the cold, their foliage dark green with the freeze. Japanese honeysuckle leaves are blackening. The crisp zinnias look windswept in their rigor mortis.

2002: Raccoon killed on Dayton-Yellow Springs road last night.

2003: Jeanie reports about a dozen turkey vultures in a tree by the riding center this morning, 8:00 a.m.

2004: Four-plus inches of snow fell overnight, making the total around sixteen inches here in Yellow Springs – the most significant accumulation in local recorded history.

2005: Cardinal singing when I went out to get wood this morning at 7:50.

2007: A sudden, hard wind blew this early morning in the dark, pushing against the house for what must have been about ten minutes. The bamboo scraped and screeched against the greenhouse wall. Heavy rain followed, rain so heavy I thought it must have been ice or sleet; checking outside, I found only the flooded sidewalk.

2008: Ice and rain this afternoon, temperatures slowly rising into the low 30s. Strong cardinal song late this morning near the yard.

2010: Snow cover continues. The oakleaf hydrangea and the knotweed have begun to lose their leaves, but the witch hazel holds its foliage tight to its wiry trunk. This afternoon, Mary Sue wrote: "Just want to let you know there was a pair of sandhill cranes hanging out at the creek and pasture on Polecat Road on the afternoon and evening of December 22 and this morning the 23rd."

2011: "Huge kettle of buzzards" reported by Ruby Nicholson at 3:50 this afternoon "near the water tower."

2012: Gethsemani, Kentucky: A mild afternoon in the 40s, gentle but steady southwest wind, cirrus and alto stratus sweeping up across the green-brown hills, groundcovers growing up because of the warm autumn, henbit and chickweed about ready to bud, just like in Yellow Springs. Black walnut hulls shriveled like some kind of arboreal scat. A few oak and American beech leaves holding on in the woods, one fern seen. Mocking birds singing occasionally, robins peeping, crows every once in a while, cardinals and blue jays seen.

2014: Mild in the upper 40s this morning. I fed the fish, and they slowly approached the surface of the water and took their food. Highs in the 50s this afternoon as I drove north to Indiana for Christmas in Goshen with the family.

2015: Mild in the 50s today, the fish still feeding. Tonight a thunderstorm with lightening all around, hard rain.

2017: The Christmas cold front approaches, the weather cooling, but the fish still swim toward me when I approach the pond.

2019: Mild in the 50s today. Robins peeping in the honeysuckles. Leslie's weekly notes becomes richer: "Domestic honeybees, hundreds out en masse in Clifton, in my sister's rewilding field where her neighbor has beehives. She and her neighbor put out plates of sugar water for the bees throughout this warm spell."

Hope and belief are easy in a warm, green world, but when the cold days come and the Sun edges farther and farther south, cutting a constantly smaller arc across the sky, the imminence of utter darkness and oblivion seems at hand. Then the Sun stands still. The turn comes. The crisis passes and the Sun slowly climbs the sky once more, reaching toward another spring, another summer.

Hal Borland

December 24th
The 358th Day of the Year

The sound was otherworldly,
an orchestra of hummingbirds
rising to crescendo.
Springing up, I shouted at my mate,
"You hear something strange?"
Up the stairs she flew.
By now the purring tremolo drone
seemed to emanate from outside
the house and overhead.

We flung open the front door and entered air
cold enough to shock our bodies alert.
She pointed: in the sky approached
divine heralds of impending birth,
a siege of sandhill cranes, wings wide,
vee-ing from the east, long necks pointing,
filling our 'hood with rhapsodic song,
shredding silence with their urgent news.
Alive. Here. Now. Shout. Rise. Fly!

The Christmas harbingers out-crowed
plagues, politics, pity, wrath and woe
with their victory lap.
Before our shouts had subsided,
they'd passed, diminuendo,
heading southwest, gone
as if they'd never been.
Back inside, we felt the echo
of their swelling motif
fill the house to bursting:
Allegro,
Annunciation.

Ed Davis, "Christmas Even Cranes"

Sunrise/set: 7:55/5:15

Day's Length: 9 hours 20 minutes
Average High/Low: 37/22
Average Temperature: 30
Record High: 66 – 1964
Record Low: -15 – 1983

The Daily Weather

Christmas Eve brings precipitation 50 percent of all the years, but a white Christmas comes more like 35 percent of the time (since sometimes that precipitation arrives in the form of rain). Although 20 percent of the days are mild in the 50s or 60s, the 24th is one of the few Ohio days in which a below-zero *high* has been recorded (in the bitter winter of 1983). Forty-five percent of the time temperatures warm to the 30s or 40s, with 20s occurring 20 percent of the afternoons, and teens on ten percent. Odds for sun are 50/50.

The Natural Calendar

On the 24th of December, the sun begins its ascent toward June, shifting from a declination of 23 degrees and 26 minutes to 23 degrees and 25 minutes. (Of course, it is Earth that actually shifts in relation to the sun.) Although the days in our village do not start to lengthen until the 26th, the 24th is the first day of the Season of the Rising Sun, a period which divides the year into two equal halves and which lasts until the sun stops at its highest point above the horizon between June 19 and 23 and then begins to fall towards winter solstice on June 24.

Milder weather in the lower Midwest may open pussy willows and draw up snowdrops, crocus and aconites as the days expand, but along the Gulf of Mexico, the Season of the Rising Sun is already shortening the dormancy of trees and shrubs, hurrying the gestation of spring. Across coastal Georgia, sweet gums and yellow poplars finally lose their leaves, and their buds swell almost immediately to replace the loss. In central Florida, red maples open, and Jessamine produces its yellow blossoms.

In my village along the 40th Parallel, the Season of Dormancy can last from November through March, but a little more than a thousand miles south, that period narrows to a slender, ambivalent space, a borderland in which the difference between winter and spring balances on a fulcrum as small as a single plant or a single hour. Along Yellow Springs Creek, the apparent movement of the sun on December 24th seems frozen in the long stillness of our landscape, but somewhere between the Marshes of Glynn and the Everglades that minute change undoes the advance of superficial cold and stirs the coals of far-off summer's core.

Daybook

1984: Geese flew over just before sundown, a little after 5:00. Hepatica reported blooming in the Glen.

1985: First striped-breasted sparrow seen at the bird feeder.

1987: One or two pussy willow catkins have cracked in the warmth. Crocuses are starting to push up through the mulch. Purple deadnettle is growing back. After dark, I surprised a flock of sparrows sleeping in the mock orange. They exploded away through the branches.

1988: Geese flew over just before sundown.

1995: After a week and a half of snow and below-freezing temperatures, dead Osage leaves finally fall from their branches (the frost had killed them in early November) and lie about on top of the snow.

1997: Rain all day and temperatures in the 40s. Judy reports a blizzard moving down from Chicago. Here the wind is gusting. Sparrows and squirrels eating sunflower seeds by the pond this gray afternoon. Downtown, a few pear leaves still hold on stubbornly. In the greenhouse, the mother-of-millions are in full bloom.

1998: The weather finally has turned cold, but I found an earthworm by the side of the road this morning. He had been driven out of his December den by yesterday's heavy rain. Now, half frozen, he was attempting to traverse a wasteland of pebbles along High Street. I knelt and took the earthworm, held him against the warmth of my palm, then set him over in the garden where the sun had heated up the ground a little. I scratched the surface of the dirt to give him a start on his descent. I covered him with grass and twigs to protect him from solar rays, and left him to make his way.

2000: Crows at 8:15 a.m. making tremendous racket in the back trees. Song sparrow noticed by the feeder. Tonight, as Jeanie and I sat with the candles lit after supper, a camelback cricket came hopping down the hall. Good luck this Christmas Eve.

2003: Returning from Goshen, Indiana, we saw only one sparrow hawk.

2007: Crows at 7:45 this morning, three large hawks seen on fences as we returned from Columbus.

2008: Almost all the pale hulls have fallen away from the bittersweet on Limestone Street and in the Limestone Street alley near Casey's house. No geese flying over town at different times of the day - they used to be a regular presence, now gone someplace else.

2009: First tufted titmouse heard about 8:00 this morning, later the red-bellied woodpecker. In the afternoon - to Columbus to pick up Neysa: a huge flock of crows on the way back from the airport, then a giant flock of starlings swooping across the freeway. The day was mild with sun in and out, the wind from the southeast tonight when I walked Bella.

2010: Mary Sue wrote this morning: "I was out in the backyard feeding the birds around eight this morning. We live next to the fields on the edge of town near Ellis Pond. I looked across the road to see if the two sandhill cranes were among the geese sitting around the area where I'd last seen them. I didn't see the cranes, then suddenly they were flying low over the geese, then over Polecat Road and over the pasture next to our house. They continued over the farm lane and landed in a field by the wood's edge. Spectacular start to Christmas Eve."

Throughout the afternoon, the chatter of birds here in town, many starlings still in the tall trees behind our house and along Dayton Street.

2011: Crows at 7:44 this morning, cold mist and fog outside. The sparrows fed heavily today. Rick wrote about seeing sandhill cranes earlier this month: "Hope you caught some of those flights of cranes coming over. One of the last ones, of about fifty flying quite high, circled our house long enough for Mary and I to run inside and put glasses on them. Seems it was around the 5th or 6th of December around three in the afternoon. When they started circling I actually tried to call you, but no answer and I ran back outside. Mary had never seen them, so was pretty excited. I liked Lauren's description of their sound, like water running over rocks."

2012: Gethsemani, Kentucky: Light rain and highs in the 40s. I took few short walks in the nearby hills, the ground covers strong and bright. Around a grotto structure at the top of one knob, hemlock had unfolded, bushy to maybe a foot tall, and great sweet rocket leaves were flopping over, lolling about almost, completely ready for spring. In the monastery walk near the bird feeders (rich with juncos, chickadees, cardinals, blue jays, titmice and a red-bellied woodpecker), I found a Lenten rose still in bloom (or blooming early) with purple flowers.

2013: Gethsemani, Kentucky: Under a holly tree filled with bright red berries, one lamium with a violet bud.

2015: Early morning at Jill's house, blanket of clouds rising up over Dayton, pushed by the warm west wind, revealing the giant round moon setting. Above Jill's back yard a little later, the moon gone, Venus so bright filling up the east. North to Goshen, Indiana, mild throughout the trip, not a single murmuration of starlings.

2016: Christmas Eve, low sky of stratus clouds, soft mist, gentle temperature in the 40s: Jill and I walked through the woods at the Indian Mound Park. We could see through bare, black trees into layers of spring: new grass at our feet and beside the path, of heavy yellow-green matted moss on decaying logs, then of swamp glades with glowing foliage of chickweed and garlic mustard and buttercups spreading among brambles to the far berm and then to the ridge beyond.

Across the ocean, Aleppo in Syria was falling to the dictator, Assad. The pain and loss of life in the city's futile defense left me confused and hopeless. I knew that human beings were evil beyond redemption. I thought about how love, as I once read, might be the only certain antidote to death. Cold comfort for the murdered children of Aleppo.

We walked up the slippery path to the ancient Adena mound, a pyramid in the once primeval forest that had most certainly cost many lives to build and to defend and then had been abandoned, perhaps overrun by enemy clans. This Christmas Eve, it stood April green, enigmatic above the wetland.

2017: A snowstorm approaches from the west as I sit in the greenhouse by the fire, a storm followed by deep cold to close out Early Winter. In Portland, Oregon, Jeni's Christmas Eve dinner for John's relatives is almost derailed by heavy snowfall. From a little north of here, Chris

Walker wrote about sighting what he thought was a Snowy Owl."Debbie and I saw a first-ever sight (for us) today. A Snowy Owl, sitting on a telephone pole in broad daylight, 30' off the right-of-way on State Route 235 up here in Champaign County.

"Debbie and I sped by the pole on the way to New Carlisle, and I just caught a passing glimpse of this large bird sitting atop the pole. Lots of white, large rounded head, some gray on its wings. As I passed I thought, 'Wait—what was that?' I turned the truck around, saying to Debbie, 'I just saw a big bird and it sure looked like a snowy owl but it can't possibly be. They're not supposed to be down here.' Driving back I thought, 'Barred Owl?' Bald eagle? A really old hawk? Barn Owl?'

"I pulled over across the road from the bird, got out, and was able to get pretty close to it. Definitely an owl. Huge and stout. Yellow eyes—not dark like a Barred Owl or a Barn Owl. Plus way too big for either. But the face was pure white, not the gray-and-white growth-ring look of a Great Gray Owl.

"Then it flew over my head, over the road, and glided silently away. It had pure white under its wings, with a heavy speckling of gray or dark brown on its sides and on the backs of its wings. Long graceful wings, almost eagle-like (and eagle-sized!!!), not stumpy like a Barred Owl. And feathered feet.

"It had to be a Snowy Owl. From the amount of markings, I'm guessing a female. But have you ever seen or heard of one this far south?"

2018: Rosemary told me that her snowdrops were up an inch and that as she was driving to Yellow Springs from Xenia she saw a bald eagle in a corn field not far from Goes Station, and the eagle had caught a rabbit, but the rabbit was too heavy for it, and the eagle was dragging it across the field. This is the third bald eagle sighting late this year, one from Casey, another from John. Leslie reports: "Tufted titmouse sings spring song, *Peter-Peter*."

2020: Gray, foggy, barometer rising, chill in the north wind, blizzard in the northern states, robins peeping in the alley, deep cold for tomorrow. Then through the barometric gorge before Christmas, the I was on the phone with my daughter Neysa in Italy when Casey called at exactly 12:00 p.m. to tell me sandhill cranes were passing over his house, and then right afterward, Anne Randolph left a message, and then Ed Davis sent an email: "Hey, Bill," wrote Ed, "two large groups of cranes just flew over Talus Drive, making their raucous, almost purring sounds, veeing toward the southwest. What a magnificent, thrilling Christmas gift in this strange year!"

And then Liz Porter: "JUST NOW! Over my house and yours! I think three chevrons of them—a huge flock! My heart is full." And then Rick Donaho: "Hey Bill, did you happen to see them just now. I'd just gotten home, putting away groceries, when I thought maybe the sump pump or something was on the blink, when something else made me run outside and sure enough, there they were, scores of cranes flying over in two or three different groups, maybe three hundred feet up, and then here came some more. What better Christmas gift for our sleepy village."

Once again at Christmas did we weave
the holly round the Christmas hearth;
the silent snow possessed the earth
and calmly fell our Christmas Eve.

Alfred Lord Tennyson

December 25th
The 359th Day of the Year

Some say that ever 'gainst that season comes
Wherein our Savior's Birth is celebrated,
The bird of dawning singeth all night long;
And then, they say, no spirit can walk abroad;
The nights are wholesome;
Then no planets strike, no fairy takes,
Nor witch hath power to charm,
So hallow'd and so gracious is the time.

William Shakespeare

Sunrise/set: 7:55/5:15
Day's Length: 9 hours 20 minutes
Average High/Low: 37/22
Average Temperature: 29
Record High: 65 – 1893
Record Low: -13 – 1983

The Daily Weather

Christmas day is generally cold and partly sunny, snow remaining on the ground three to four years in ten. The arrival of the fifth high pressure system of the month often brings storms or flurries. Chances of highs in the 50s or 60s are 15 percent. Forties come another 15 percent of the time, 30s about 40 percent, 20s or below 30 percent. One Christmas in a quarter century remains below zero. The sun appears a little more than half of all the years.

Natural Calendar

Sometimes a fat camel cricket will emerge in the kitchen at night, searching for crumbs. In the chicken house, pullets that will produce summer eggs are hatching. In the warmth of greenhouses, bedding plants scheduled to be sold in April and May could have four to six leaves.

1982: Record warm temperatures throughout the East and Midwest, 63 in Yellow Springs. Mint found half a foot high in Mint Hollow.

1983: Record cold. Ellis Pond was frozen, the first time I've seen it like that since we came in 1978. Two boys were playing on the ice. Geese were huddled together at the far shore.

1985: Geese were restless this morning. I could hear them flying near Ellis Pond.

1990: Splitting Osage at sunset, half moon and Aldebaran in the orange sky, temperatures into the teens, and my breath white, I feel like I'm closing in on the rhythm. I feel that everything could be right here in front of me. I felt the same way after I read Kiser's fishing and weather journal, his plain, simple entries, life reduced to this and that. Everything I need is right in front of me. Limits are clear and distinct this cold Christmas evening. Things mean what they are. I don't need myths, allegories, metaphors. These are the same stars and moon that shone on Bethlehem. Jesus must be here beside me.

1991: A cardinal sang in the dark, maybe half an hour before dawn.

1995: Six inches of snow on the ground, gentle flurries all day accumulating a little on the shoveled sidewalk. The Christmas cold front approaches on schedule, the windows frosting up.

1997: A crow passed through the yard at 7:35 a.m. A cardinal sang for almost a minute at 8:30 a.m. After yesterday's two-inch rain, the land is soft. A worm was forced out of the ground, drowned in a puddle. The koi in the pond were given a Christmas meal: they rose to the top to feed for the first time in maybe six weeks.

2003: A small flock of crows flew southeast over the house about 8:00 a.m.

2004: Eight below zero on the 24th, ten below this morning, the coldest Christmas Eve and Christmas in many years.

2006: A mild December and days of rain have brought the snowdrops and daffodils up two inches in the front garden.

2007: Crows at 7:45 a.m. No cardinals heard in a long time. Clear and chilly this morning, mild this afternoon. Tat says 28 inches of snow are on the ground in Madison, but the grass is green and bare a hundred miles south at Judy's house in Goshen, Indiana.

2008: The sky clear and brightening at 7:00 when I went outside. Crows at 7:45. The sun was warm and comforting when Bella and I walked the alley around noon.

2009: I got up about 5:00 this morning in the middle of a Christmas rainstorm, the wind and raindrops pelting the southeast corner of the house. I sat for almost an hour listening to the waves and eddies of the storm. I built up the fire, and the wind whistled and moaned in the cracks around the stove door. After an hour, the rain stopped, but the wind kept on, and by sunrise, Yellow Springs lay in the center of the low-pressure cell, the sky clearing.

Then when I went outside, I found a *Polygonia comma*, an angel-wing butterfly, on the head of the stone crucifix Tat had given us some years ago. It had apparently emerged or was driven from its winter quarters in the storm and had found refuge on the cross. The *polygonias* overwinter as adults, so I thought it might have a chance to survive the coming cold. I watched it all day as the temperature held steady in the 40s. I went out before bed, and it was still there, the temperature dipping toward 30.

2010: Crows at 7:37 this morning, and the steady sound of robins around 8:30. Half a dozen juncos seen near the back feeder around noon today, working the outer perimeter of the area. And late in the afternoon, two dark cowbirds scratched for seeds, pushing out the sparrows. The robins and the cowbirds may have come in with the starlings. Were the juncos with them?

2011: Crows at 7:30 this morning, the sky clear and bright. Clouds moved in off and on through the day.

2012: Gethsemani: Low clouds across the gray hills, birds feeding heavily. North in Yellow Springs, a winter storm warning is in effect, and I wonder about the plants in the greenhouse tonight.

2015: Goshen, Indiana: Sun and 40s, high, wispy cirrus, walked around the park lake without my coat on, hundreds of geese on the open water, sandhill cranes heard far to the north. Record warmth and rain across the east coast. Jill sent a photo from Washington, D.C. of two pink roses blooming.

2017: Deep cold throughout the Midwest, Jill and I drove to Goshen against a hard wind and blowing snow. Single digits tonight.

2019: Drove to Goshen, Indiana, sunny and temperature in the 50s throughout the day, the entire eastern half of the country mild, the Christmas front nowhere in sight. Two large hawks noticed on the drive. Leslie finds a green ladybird beetle, "probably Genus *Psyllobora*." She also heard house finches and tufted titmice in full spring song.

2020: Lows in the teens this morning, barometer slowly rising, and at 10:38, I received a call from Casey: "Get outside!" he said, "They're comin' your way." And Jill and I ran out the front door to hear sandhill cranes in the clouds above us, their soft guttural gobbling moving to the south. This noon, a flock of fat starlings swarming in the yard. Later, Audrey and Grant wrote: "At 12:12 in the afternoon, we saw a flock of maybe 40 fly right over our house, headed south down High Street. They flew so low, we could see their feathers ad feet. Their rattle-calls, too, were thrillingly close and clear."

Perhaps what most moves us in winter is some reminiscence of far-off summer.... The cold is merely superficial; it is summer still at the core, far, far within.

Henry David Thoreau, *Journal*, January 12, 1855

December 26th
The 360th Day of the Year

The cycle of time is born again.
The months begin their march.
The earth will give its gifts untilled,
Wandering ivy, foxglove, colocasia, laughing acanthus.
Untended she-goats freely bear their milk.
The snake and poison plant will perish,
The plains turn gold with corn.
Grapes will redden on the briar.
Oaks will drip with honey.

Virgil

Sunrise/set: 7:55/5:16
Day's Length: 9 hours 21 minutes
Average High/Low: 37/22
Average Temperature: 29
Record High: 66 – 2016; 62 – 1889
Record Low: - 6 – 1983

The Daily Weather
The 26th brings highs in the 50s or 60s ten percent of the time, 40s thirty percent of the time, highs in the 30s on 30 percent of the afternoons, 20s twenty percent, and teens on the remaining ten percent. Skies are completely cloudy two years out of three on this date. Snow falls a third of the time, but rain is rare. Chances of a morning below zero are 20 percent, 90 percent for a morning below freezing.

The Weather in the Week Ahead
The last days of the year are typically dominated by the Christmas cold front, which chills the 26th and 27th, then moderates as it moves east, bringing a 40 percent chance of highs in the 40s or above. After the passage of the January 1 weather system, highs remain below 40 on 80 percent of the afternoons. The likelihood of precipitation increases as the old year fades. From a 35 percent

149

chance of rain or snow on the 27th, chances increase to a 55 percent chance on the 31st.

Natural Calendar

Along the 40th Parallel, the rate at which sunset becomes later now outstrips the rate at which sunrise becomes later, and the days start to lengthen on the 26th; they will continue to grow at the rate of about seven minutes a week until January 15th. After that, night recedes a little better than two minutes every day all the way to early summer.

Daybook

1982: Mint is five inches high in parts of the garden patch.

1983: Most rivers are frozen. Skaters have been out on the ice behind the Grinnell Mill dam.

1985: Yellow Springs Creek is frozen in places. Two weeks of early Deep Winter have hurt the watercress at Jacoby, but the ragwort is still holding.

1986: No cardinals heard today, but I saw a very large flock of crows along the Xenia highway.

1987: Fishing with dough balls north of Jacoby this morning, no bites at all. The woods was quiet except for a few crows. I saw a pair of ducks upriver. At home, sparrows were all over the honeysuckles, sang all afternoon.

1988: Jacoby Swamp: With all the ice, it was easy to walk across to the cattails from where the cowslips had bloomed in April. Foliage of the dock, leafcup, buttercups and ragwort was burned and limp from the cold, but the watercress was still bright green – even when it was frozen solid in the streams. Red rose hips stood out against the white sycamore bark. A whip-poor-will sang on the other side of the road. Two kingfishers came screaming down the river. I saw one mallard, new mint, Osage fruits broken apart by squirrels, empty milkweed pods, and a honeybee drowned in the pond. At home, crocus spears have come up behind the garden wall.

1989: A cardinal heard today, 11:55 a.m. Just one more month until they begin to sing before dawn.

1992: No crows seen in Springfield. Occasional flocks of starlings noticed as I drove through Indiana.

1997: North to Goshen in northern Indiana. Flocks of crows and swarms starlings on the five-hour drive. The sky: *Stratus opacus uniformis* from Yellow Springs all the wayto northern Indiana. Occasionally some *undulatus* visible. Patches of pale green winter wheat gave the land its only spring color.

2003: To South Glen at 9:00 a.m. The sun was rising over the river, the sky was pale blue, the woods golden in the morning, the river high and dark, the ground mottled with leaves and snow. As soon as I approached Sycamore Hole, a flock of maybe a dozen mallards flew off quacking. As I walked west down the path, I was surrounded by continuous cardinal song, the rattling of woodpeckers, the distant call of crows and the cackling of starlings, the chirping of a few sparrows, the chatter of a downy woodpecker. When I came home, I saw a robin in the front yard peeping, and a large flock of crows flew south over the house a little before sundown.

2004: Casey called about 9:30 this morning, told me to go out and look in the southeast: "There're three sundogs!" he said. And I went out with the phone in my hand, and he directed me almost overhead to the first half rainbow, then lower, a second, smaller sundog. The third was a bright spot in the clouds right above the sun. "Lordy be!" joked Casey. "What kind of year are we going to have!" Even though he was joking, there was something in his voice that betrayed a sense of awe and trepidation.

2006: Doves heard calling in the mild 40-degree morning.

2007: Crows came by at 7:30 and 7:45 this morning, the sky above clear, a ragged bank of gray alto stratus clouds in the east, Venus over them in the southeast.

2008: A storm at midday, gentle, rolling thunder in the south, steady rain. Ice kept Judy and Tat from shopping in Goshen, Indiana.

2009: I checked the butterfly *(Polygonia nativitatis)* on the crucifix this morning: it was still there, the sky clearing, wind still up, barometer only a little higher than yesterday. At 7:30, a long "V" of geese flew over the house. At 8:00, crows skirted the west woodlot. Throughout the morning, strong sun into the greenhouse, clarity and warmth. I've heard no cardinals for what seems like months. Saw Rick at the grocery store; he said he had seen a large flock of robins yesterday, acting like they were migrating, peeping and heading south through the woods.

2010: Crows at 7:35 this morning. Wind picking up, major storm heading up the East coast from the Carolinas.

2012: Gethsemani: A fierce storm is sweeping across the Lower Midwest, throwing half a foot of snow on Yellow Springs, moving to bring a foot or more on Janie up in New Hampshire. In the Deep South, tornadoes. Here in Gethsemani, clouds, fog, rain, flurries, northwest wind.

2013: Gethsemani: Cloudless sky, high in the 40s: I walked to Fredric's Lake, saw a bluebird and a flock of robins (peeping and peeping) and one scrawny dandelion peeking out from the gravel path.

2017: Deep cold near zero continues. The temperature in the greenhouse dips into the upper 40s at night, climbs into the middle 50s with sun by noon. The Christmas cacti remain in full bloom, and geraniums are still flowering, but almost all the vincas have stopped blossoming, will start up again, I am guessing, as soon as the days lengthen and the room warms. The plumeria trees have yellowed/ocher leaves now, will lose most of them within a month or so and then start growing new foliage. Jill's friend, Lois, is stranded in her motel in Erie, Pennsylvania, where record lake-effect snow of over 60 inches has paralyzed movement in and out of the city.

2019: Home from Goshen, warm near 60 degrees through the day.

This evening near sundown at Ellis, the great flock of geese is in full symphonic voice, screeching and bellowing, smaller groups flying back and forth, calling. Dozens of starlings visit Leslie's property. Honeybees continue to feed on sugar water at Jennifer's place in Clifton.

2020: Bright sun, low in the teens, barometer steady at 30.0, stable after yesterday's rise. Jill sends a note at 10:45: A big flock of starlings landed in her yard. Then at 12:08, John Blakelock called, "Sandhill cranes! They should be right over your house!" I ran out, and there they were east of High Street circling the center of town. Then when I went inside, Marianne MacQueen called: She and Pam Conine had just seen a flock of 40 sandhill cranes, and while I was on the phone with Marianne, a got a message from Anne Randolph: a flock of 30 or 40 was passing right over her house on Stuart Street. Then at 12:55, Betty Ross called: Another flock was coming over High Street toward Whiteman Street. Audrey and Grant heard them: "There seemed to be two flocks this time, much further away and so just barely visible. 'Tis the season for sandhill cranes!"

The south-wind searches for the flowers whose
fragrance late he bore,
And sighs to find them in the woods and by the
stream no more.

William Cullen Bryant

December 27th
The 361st Day of the Year

O Winter, ruler of the inverted year...
I crown thee King of intimate delights,
Fireside enjoyments, homeborn happiness.

William Cowper

Sunrise/set: 7:56/5:17
Day's Length: 9 hours 21 minutes
Average High/Low: 36/21
Average Temperature: 29
Record High: 66 – 2008
Record Low: - 4 – 1950

The Daily Weather
A slight warming trend begins today four years in ten, and it sometimes continues until the 1st of January. On the 27th and 28th, highs reach the 50s or 60s twenty-five percent of the time, and below-zero lows are rare. Colder weather is certainly not unusual for this date, however. Twenty percent of the days are in the 40s, forty percent are in the 30s, and another 20 percent in the 20s or teens. Clouds continue to dominate the sky, and snow or sleet comes 35 percent of the days.

Natural Calendar
The hydrangea heads are drooping, and the Jerusalem artichokes have fallen over. Grasses are pale and bent. Hoary goldenrod and brittle great ragweed have broken. Chicory stalks are leaning. Pokeweed, hollow and empty, rattles in the wind. The snow and the overwintering robins pull off the last honeysuckle berries. Winterberry branches are bending to let down their fruit. Bittersweet hulls continue to split away from their branches. The evergreen foliage of the hardiest herbs and flowers collapses tight against the frozen but nurturing ground: Sweet rocket, garlic mustard, ragwort, celandine, poppies, thistles, chives and parsley crouch in wait like new seeds for the Shining Grackle Moon of February and the Singing

Toad Moon of March.

The Stars

An hour before sunrise, Orion has set. Sirius has moved deep into the west, Cancer and Gemini following it. The Big Dipper is overhead. June's Arcturus is coming in from the east, and August's Vega has risen in the northeast.

Daybook

1987: At Sycamore Hole, a small shiner caught on every cast. No sound in the woods until the middle of the afternoon, then one cardinal sang.

1988: A cardinal sang three or four times this warm and sunny afternoon. The columbine against the south wall grew a new leaf. Forget-me-nots, mint, wild onion, henbit, moneywort, clover, celandine, plantain, dock, ragwort were all thick and lush. Crocus was up more than an inch. Some pussy willows were breaking out.

1989: Some of the photographs taped to my notebook remind me of the exhilaration I felt on my walks, the brilliant greens of the cress, fog along the high river, the broken trees at Jacoby swamp, black from the rain, all of the contrasts so intense, my own excitement inseparable from those colors and contrasts, and I laugh because I can't believe it is making me so happy now, the thought of the exquisitely gloomy, cold wetland.

1992: A few cabbages still alive and firm in the garden. Geese flew over the south end of town at sunset.

1995: I picked a pussy willow branch picked to use as a model for sketching, the buds tight and red.

1997: After light flurries, the stratus clouds break up, become a variety of cumulus, stratocumulus, nimbostratus, altostratus. Then the nimbostratus dominate, and there is a little rain and wet snow.

1999: Stubborn snapdragons and Japanese honeysuckles are finally giving in, blackening with the cold.

2003: The jade trees in the greenhouse are still in full bloom. The purple wandering Jews are budding. As I let Bella out the back door before sunrise, I heard a cardinal singing. Walking the dog later, I heard sparrows chirping, starlings whistling. On their early walk, Jeanie and Dianne counted 40 buzzards by the riding center about 8:00 a.m. – obviously part of the migration did not take place. And the past several years have produced vulture sightings deep into November.

2004: Cardinals singing off and on throughout the thaw, accentuating the increase in their songs during December this year. Is this a complement to the buzzards staying year round? Along the hedge, the Japanese honeysuckle has been blackened by the Christmas cold.

2005: Early December's cold has given way to thaw. The old season had been covered and sealed; now with the snow gone, the land has been transformed. Mild midwinter temperatures reveal a gateway to spring.

In many ways, nothing has changed over the past few weeks. The trees are still bare, and no new sprouts have appeared in the undergrowth. Pussy willow catkins are thin and tight. Forsythia buds show no hint of their February blush.

Autumn's fruits, however, are giving way to the weather, measuring the advance of the Northern Hemisphere back toward the sun. The feathery heads of virgin's bower, soft and thick in late November, have blown away in the wind. The hosta pods are almost empty. The final rose of Sharon seeds lie precariously in their open calices. Worn tufts of ironweed are half gone.

The heads of purple coneflowers and zinnias, tough and unyielding a month ago, crumble between my fingers. Honeysuckle and euonymus berries still hang to their branches, but their flush and firmness are gone. In the greenhouse, the fall blossoms have withered on the Christmas cacti. The flowers are done blooming on one jade tree, starting to decline on the other.

As the thaw deepens, remnants of the past year no longer point to the warmth of last October. The sharp yucca, tall and bright green, does not look back to June, but forward to June. In the pond, wild iris spears that braved weeks of ice stand strong around the broken strands of lizard's tail. As the bamboo in the south garden recovers from the weight of the snow, it shows sweet rockets, henbit, great mullein, celandine, wild lettuce, dock, sweet Williams and lamb's ear waiting for April and May.

2007: Rain and mild this morning, crows sleeping in a bit, fly over at about five to eight. A rose-breasted nuthatch seen briefly at the east garden feeder while we were having lunch with Neysa and Sebastian.

2008: Walked in the alley at 9:00 this morning, south wind, temperature at 60 degrees, heading for a record high. Robins peeping throughout the neighborhood as if roused from their overwintering to hunt worms in the warming soil or to gorge themselves on the very last honeysuckle berries. A long "V" of geese flew over the schoolyard at about 9:30.

In the Stafford Street alley, tall coneflower stalks have collapsed around the telephone pole. In my south garden, the false boneset has toppled over, and the small white asters, their seed heads empty, are leaning toward the aging Osage fruits. In the pond, the swamp rushes lie with the lizard's tail flat across the water.

We drove to Goshen, Indiana in the afternoon with a strong southwest wind that kept temperatures in the 60s throughout the trip. A few miles south of Goshen, we hit dark clouds and heavy rain.

2009: Sun this morning through layers of cirrus and altostratus and low fragments of stratus. We went out to shop, and by the middle of the afternoon the sky was gray, snow starting at about 6:00, around two inches when it was all over. Cathy writes from Vermont: "There is a herd of blue jays that come thundering into our side yard every morning."

2010: Steady wind through the night. Crows heard late at 7:50. Mary Sue sends more information about the sandhill cranes near Ellis Pond: "At mid-day on Christmas Eve, Peter and I walked up the farm lane by the cornfields (between the woods and Ellis Pond) and followed the cranes through the field for a good while. Got a few more good photos. Didn't have time to look for them again until this morning. They had roosted overnight in the same spot as the first evening I saw them. I patiently watched from a window until they finally stirred up and flew to the cornfield again."

2012: Gethsemani, Kentucky: Gray and cold today, flurries but the snow did not stick. The storm has gone into the Northeast, leaving us quiet. The wind stays firm from the northwest, crows came by at 7:50, about the same time they do at home.

2013: From Gethsemani to Yellow Springs: Not a single starling flock seen on my drives to and from Kentucky. Only a few vultures circled the road toward Cincinnati.

2014: I came home from Indiana to find a large camel cricket in the bathtub.

2015: From Washington, D.C., Jill sent photos of forsythia, iris, hellebores, roses and what appear to be pachysandra in full bloom.

2016: Record warmth from the Mississippi east, but it isn't bringing the flowers into bloom like last year.

2018: Goshen, Indiana: Thousands of geese congregating at the ponds.

2019: Mild weather continues, robins peeping.

2020: Sun and mild after several days of cold and snow, the barometer steady and drifting down, the Christmas cold front canyon leveling off.

Journal

Waiting for spring can be like trying to go to sleep when you have insomnia. Sometimes the best thing to do is to count. Counting is a simple measure of time, limits time to individual pieces, takes away its mystery and emptiness. Counting is an act of will, forces focus, works against discouragement, places the counter in opposition to the psychology and physiology of sleeplessness.

Numbers are infinite, and so are the pieces of winter. Counting in sequence creates apparent progress and finite limits. Even though awareness of winter's events seems to produce few results, seems to have no sum or substance, observations can be like digits in a sprawling but promising night time equation, the fruit of persistence and dogged hope.

Like counting sheep or breaths or numerals, counting dimensions of the interval between autumn and April requires no rules or ethics, is not competitive, does not require special study or skill. Like counting sheep or breaths or numerals, the choice of things to be counted is arbitrary, has no necessary socially redeeming value, does not end poverty or bring peace, has no theology. This is the anarchy, the freedom of mindfulness that looses the mind's eye to rhythm or accumulation or listing or repetition or the emptiness of any single object until something new suddenly occurs without our creating it and we fall asleep and dream, or become fully awake and discover spring.

The Sun swings slowly north, in our way of seeing it; days lengthen; the season of life renewed, which we call Spring is already established in the earth as among the stars.

Hal Borland

December 28th
The 362nd Day of the Year

In winter the stars seem to have rekindled their fires, the moon achieves a fuller triumph, and the heavens wear a look of a more exalted simplicity. Summer is more wooing and seductive, more versatile and human, appeals to the affections and sentiments and fosters inquiry and the art impulse. Winter is of a more heroic cast, and addresses the intellect. The severe studies and disciplines come easier in winter. One imposes larger tasks upon himself, and is less tolerant of his own weaknesses.

John Burroughs

Sunrise/set: 7:56/5:17
Day's Length: 9 hours 21 minutes
Average High/Low: 36/21
Average Temperature: 29
Record High: 63 – 1996
Record Low: - 6 – 1924

The Daily Weather

Chances of highs in the 50s or 60s are 15 percent; mild 40s occur 30 percent of the days, and afternoons in the 30s come on 45 percent, leaving very little room for severe weather. The sky is almost always cloudy on the 28th, and there is just a 30 percent chance of even partly sunny conditions. Rain is more frequent than snow, falling 20 percent of the time; flurries occur just five to ten percent of the time.

Natural Calendar

New daffodil, crocus, and tulip leaves lie just below the surface of the mulch. Dock, leafcup, buttercup, mint, ragwort, sweet rocket, plantain, thistles, great mullein, moneywort, red clover, celandine, forget-me-not, wild onion, purple deadnettle, and henbit foliage push every-so-gradually toward March. Deep in the woods, the earthstar fungus, shaped like a six-pointed star, appears. Multiflora rose buds swell in the sun.

161

1982: Crocus growing after a warm spell. Foliage of the pansies and primroses, wild mallow, mint, wild onion, ivy, moneywort, clover, plantain, celandine continues to thrive. A few pussy willows are emerging.

1988: A warm late December like 1982; columbine in the yard even growing a new leaf.

1996: Highs were in the 60s today. Jeanie and I went for a bike ride down to Antioch School, and this afternoon I worked outside until supper. There was even sun to go along with the mild temperatures! At five o'clock, as I stood in the door of the workshop, I saw a tan moth fluttering around the woodpile. Tonight, a fat camel cricket went jumping across the kitchen floor. In the garden, the chives I transplanted toward the end of last month seem to have died, but the garlic cloves planted at the same time are sending down roots.

1997: A few rust-colored leaves still hold to the beech tree, but the pears are finally completely bare.

2002: A long hard cardinal song in the gray morning, temperature 30 degrees. Then silence.

2003: A sunny and mild day. Sparrows were chirping when I walked Bella this morning. I saw a flock of crows crossing the freeway as I drove to Columbus early this afternoon.

2005: Thunder this morning about 7:00. A flock of robins in the yard at 10:30. The sun was out for a while, highs into the middle 50s.

2006: Titmouse heard for several mornings now. Doves seen in the back trees, maybe paired for spring?

2007: Crows at 7:45 a.m. once again. Sparrows, chickadees and cardinals about, but no birdsong in the mornings.

2008: Between Goshen, Indiana and Yellow Springs: Only one flock of starlings, one large hawk.

2009: Fresh rosemary picked from the garden for Neysa's lamb soup.

2010: New York continues to be snowed in, and Moscow's airport is shut down because of the weather. California is still being battered by heavy rains, heavy snows and high winds.

2011: A chilly, windswept day, cumulus clouds out of the northwest, sun and shade, cold and mild. Ruth Paige called to report sandhill cranes flying over the south end of town at a little after 3:00 p.m. Ruby reported "one buzzard feeding on the road side." Both observations significant because they could not have been made a decade ago.

2012: Long walk at Gethsemani, hills green, ground ivy starting to rise, budded.

2013: At South Glen, almost 50 degrees, chickweed spreading, even where the river had flooded after the snow melted and then the rains came. Robins peeping in the woods and in town.

2014: At South Glen, windy, high 30s, land dun and pale yellow-green, chickweed spreading. Only one crow heard; then, on my way back after an hour walk, three Eastern bluebirds flew in front of me toward the river.

2015: All-day rain in Yellow Springs, windy and icing in Goshen, Indiana, Winter Storm Goliath paralyzes the lower Plains.

2017: Deep cold, but barometer dropping in advance of the Supermoon and deeper cold with snow. John Blakelock called at 12:41 in the afternoon: "I just saw a flock of about thirty or forty cranes above the junction of I-675 and Dayton-Yellow Springs Road, and they were heading straight south." He thought they were the stragglers from two weeks ago that were finally admitting that winter wouldn't wait any longer.

2018: Drive from Goshen, Indiana to Yellow Springs: Two sparrow hawks, several murmurations of starlings noticed. Mild temperatures in the 40s throughout the Lower Midwest and the East. Casey called to report he had seen a bluebird this afternoon.

When Christmas is ended, bid feasting adieu,
go play the good husband, the stock to renew.
Be mindful of rearing in hope of a gain,
dame profit shall give thee reward for thy pain.

Thomas Tusser, 16th Century

December 29th
The 363rd Day of the Year

Full knee-deep lies the winter snow,
And the winter winds are wearily sighing.
Toll ye the church-bell sad and slow,
And tread softly and speak low,
For the old year lies a-dying.

Alfred Lord Tennyson

Sunrise/set: 7:56/5:18
Day's Length: 9 hours 22 minutes
Average High/Low: 36/21
Average Temperature: 28
Record High: 68 – 1889
Record Low: - 5 – 1983

The Daily Weather
There is a 15 percent chance of a high in the 60s today, 15 percent for 50s, fifteen percent for 40s, thirty-five percent for 30s, fifteen percent for 20s, five percent for teens. The sun appears on four days in ten, and precipitation, most often in the form of rain across southwestern Ohio, occurs one day in three.

Natural Calendar
As the weather gets colder, wild game moves to areas where cover is thickest. For deer, mating season is over. White-tailed bucks have their gray winter coats now, and they are starting to drop their antlers. On the farm, expectant ewes, does and cows nurture their babies to be born a few weeks from now in late winter or early spring. In the fields around Yellow Springs, geese continue to gather.

Daybook
1983: The deep cold has turned the Japanese honeysuckle black. All the leaves have dropped from the forsythia. Doves and sparrows huddle in the frozen garden.

1986: First striped breasted sparrow seen (song sparrow). They are rare here in Yellow Springs, show up only occasionally at the winter feeders.

1988: The sun comes up over the Yellow Springs horizon at 8:20 a.m., 25 minutes after its official rising time. I can first see it at an azimuth of about 120 degrees, east-southeast. From the front door, it appears right at the far edge of the Danielsons' roof. At noon, it lies over Nate's chimney at 170 degrees, not quite due south. It disappears into the crook of the corner Osage tree, 240 degrees, at 5:01 p.m.

1996: In the greenhouse, whiteflies have taken over the tomatoes, and spider mites eat the impatiens. There is chaos in the plantings, as much decay as growth, Christmas cacti are still blooming, but so many of the plants have withered from root disease or insects. January brings the clearing out, the leaving behind of last summer's plants, the starting of the new.

1998: Barometer dropping, rain off and on. The ice has melted on the surface of the pond, the heater no longer needed. The bird feeders have been empty for a while; only one squirrel came to check for food. Mother-of-millions still haven't flowered, but their buds are big. The Christmas cacti are done, all but a few blossoms withered. Whiteflies held in check by regular spraying. The tomatoes in the greenhouse are strong: I have enough to give away or enough for spaghetti sauce. Chard and peppers also hold well so far.

2003: A soft, cloudy morning, temperature near 50 degrees, barometer dropping, rain on the way. A cardinal singing and starlings chirping when I went outside about 8:30.

2006: Walking Bella at 8:30 this warm morning, I saw robins, heard titmice and cardinals calling steadily.

2007: Crows at 8:15 this morning, the sky gray and the air chilly and damp. The landscape has become sodden from the recent thaws and rains, part spring, part Late Fall, the grass greening, the fallen leaves darkening, Osage fruits becoming speckled with age, coralberries becoming paler, bittersweet hulls almost all fallen, the orange berries looking like honeysuckle berries now.

2008: A cardinal sang at 10:30 this morning. I am hearing them more often now.

2009: Titmice were singing about 8:30, but the polygonia butterfly that arrived in the Christmas storm and perched on the head of the crucifix on the 25th, 26th, 27th and 28th was gone when I went out to the porch this morning.

2010: The thaw is due to begin today. Walking into the back yard this morning was like walking into spring: peeping robins all over, starlings high in the trees, whistling and chirping, sparrows chattering. Mary Sue is still finding sandhill cranes out near Ellis Pond.

2011: Euonymus berry hulls have darkened, red fruit hanging loose. About a fourth of the pussy willows have cracked. Cardinals sing on and off throughout the morning - several males and females coming to the feeders.

2012: Gethsemani: After flurries through the night, the land was covered with snow, pines drooping, hills pure and white.

2015: To Yellow Springs from Goshen, Indiana: Many fields flooded after heavy Christmas rains; winter wheat fields bright green, even under the dull sky; no flocks of birds seen or heard; arriving home, I found the deep red hellebores had fully opened, several branches of forsythia were in bloom, snowdrops had climbed another inch, daffodils and hyacinths were pushing out from the circle garden, and snow crocus foliage looked like it was about to graduate to buds. Jill and I walked at Clifton Gorge, found one hepatica with a white blossom. Below us, the river was raging. In the evening, Matt sent two photos of cherry trees blooming in Washington, D.C.

2019: Mild 60s and light rain throughout the day. More geese seem to be arriving at Ellis each day. Leslie reports white-throated sparrow singing its full spring song.

2020: Chris Walker reports hearing the first great horned owl of the season. "A welcome return," he writes.

Love to daily uses wed
Shall be sweetly perfected.
Life by repetition grows
Unto its appointed close:
Day to day fulfills one year.

Francis Thompson

December 30th
The 364th Day of the Year

Ring out wild bells, to the wild sky,
The flying cloud, the frosty night:
The year is dying in the night;
Ring out, wild bells, and let him die.
.....
Ring out the old, ring in the new,
Ring happy bells, across the snow:
The year is going, let him go.

Alfred Lord Tennyson

Sunrise/set: 7:56/5:19
Day's Length: 9 hours 23 minutes
Average High/Low: 36/21
Average Temperature: 28
Record High: 63 – 1972
Record Low: - 9 – 1983

The Daily Weather
Highs in the 60s come five percent of the time, 50s come another five percent, 40s thirty percent, 30s forty percent, 20s ten percent, teens five percent, single digits five percent. Today is partly sunny two years out of three, but rain or snow occurs half of all the days in my record. Lows fall below freezing 55 percent of the nights, and below-zero temperatures occur one night in 20.

Natural Calendar
The heating season in the Lower Midwest typically lasts from the middle of October through the middle of April, depending on the character of the year. The cold is created by approximately 37 major cold fronts passing through the region between the third week of October and the third week of April. By today, 17 of those fronts have normally arrived, almost half the season.

Daybook

1987: A cardinal sang at 8:18 a.m. and then was quiet.

1988: A cardinal sang in the middle of the afternoon. First song sparrow seen today, a day later than in 1986.

1990: After a month of record rainfall, the river is as high as it's been in more than a quarter century. At Sycamore Hole, water is up to the path and into South Glen: maybe five to ten feet above its normal level. Access to the Covered Bridge is closed off. At the mill, the flooding came up to the underside of the footbridge by the dam. A year and a half ago, drought with no relief in sight. In the greenhouse, the Shirley tomatoes have reached ten feet - this is the best year ever for tomatoes, no major disease or insect problems, and the yield the strongest ever. The aloe flowers are gone; the last fell after Christmas. A couple of zinnias from September hold on. The parsley and chard are fresh and tender.

1991: Hyacinths up maybe an inch for several weeks now. One of them has been destroyed by squirrels digging.

1992: To a quilt exhibition in Columbus in the rain, 56 degrees. The theme of the show was gardens. All the comments by the quilters reminded me of Frances Hurie, her sorting and collecting, her perennial garden, the passion to be surrounded by patterns and intricate order, complex design which loses its coherence if approached too closely. Quilting shows a wise awareness; its squares are like days, acts that finally display their meaning or their disarray in time. Home by 4:30; while we were gone, a yellow pansy bloomed in the east garden by the front walk.

1995: At dawn, the gigantic high-pressure system that had come in after Christmas was moving off, barometer dropping, sky clear except for rose and gold cirrus in the east. Snow has covered the ground for 12 days now. Standing in the yard, I heard a cardinal singing. Birds were active at the feeder, even a huge flicker - the first time I've seen one here in years. Steady increase in clouds through the morning, thickening of cirrus and altocumulus.

    After lunch, the temperature rose past the freezing mark for the first time in a week, and I went down to the Covered Bridge with Fergus and Buttercup. The snow softened, was easily packed into snowballs. Low afternoon sun filtered through the now thick filter of altostratus, the landscape dappled with shades of grays and blacks and browns, the river frozen in some places especially along the shore, the main channels open and dark. Some leaves unhurt on a few multiflora rose bushes. A lot of sycamore leaves hold along Corey Street, but many of them lie in the snow, brought down by last week's cold. Home in the greenhouse, mother-of-millions still not blooming.

1998: Mother-of-millions budding, still not blooming.

2001: A large flock of starlings came to Susi's tree around 11:00 this morning.

2003: Returning from Goshen, we saw two road kills (raccoons) the only ones in both our trips north and back, 400 miles round trip.

2004: The skunk remains cloistered under the house, its odor vague, pervasive. Traps by the entrances remain untouched. In the greenhouse, the jade tree blossoms are getting old, a few withering. Several small flocks of starlings seen eating crabapples throughout town – and at the new tree in the front yard.

2006: A screech owl was calling this morning when I opened the back door at 6:35. Walking the dog at few hours later, I was surrounded by the songs of robins, starlings, sparrows, cardinals, doves and titmice. I stopped to talk with Peggy, who said she'd never seen so many robins in winter. I felt the same way – I've seen overwintering flocks in Yellow Springs for years, but the number of robins that seems different this year.

Thanks to a mild December, snowdrops and a few daffodils are up at least two inches in the yard. Small new hollyhock leaves have opened in the garden. Purple deadnettle has expanded into mounds under the grape arbor. Along the sidewalk, about a dozen pussy willows have cracked a little. By the trellis, honeysuckle berries, which sometimes measure the advance of spring as they disappear, are completely gone.

At the Covered Bridge, I found foot-long growth of feathery

hemlock leaves. Some rose hips were soft and squashy; some were brown, brittle, hollow. Osage fruits, some reddish, some still yellow, had been shredded by squirrels or raccoons, lay all about the forest floor.

The deeper I went into the South Glen, the more I noticed the moss around me, and I realized that almost all the stones were green, that the fallen logs were green, that the rotting stumps were green, that the oldest trees overhanging the river were covered with the thickest, most luxurious green moss, fat and bushy, an inch thick in places. Dry streambeds were filled with green rocks and branches. Limestone boulders were dripping with moss, bearded with moss, speckled with sedum and lichens. Everywhere I looked the moss offered islands of summer through the dead leaves, and it drew my vision through vertical pillars of green up into the blue sky.

This Christmas season, I have been reading essays by theologians Thomas Merton and St. Bernard. Both of them obsessively extracted novel and often useful meanings from the events of the Christian liturgical year. St. Bernard was especially gifted of at enumerating things such as the three aspects of Advent or the twelve rungs on the ladder of humility. In his lists, he explored so many unlikely dimensions of a topic, often reaching well beyond the expected to achieve his desired number of insights.

As I walked, I wondered what Bernard would do with all these green Scriptures. He was a man who made tiers of everything, filled in the empty spaces of events, created sequences out of concepts, found allegory wherever he looked. I imagined him without his Jesus and without his Church, helping me to see what really lay before me. I imagined him building the green ladder of this day, finding four transcendent stages in Glen Helen Deep Winter, six hidden levels in the thickness of mosses, nine miraculous shades of January jade, twelve secret dimensions of the living stones nestled among decaying leaves, fifteen lessons in the enigmatic deer paths that cut carpets of bright chickweed into geometric icons, twenty symbols of inner life growing from the ancient tree stumps, thirty signs of resurrection in the crossed branches of the hoary sycamores, all the meanings I needed flowering from Gaia's Word.

2007: I heard a cardinal on my walk with Bella this morning, for the first time in months. Crows heard late, about 8:15 this morning; a giant overwintering murder of crows seen along the freeway east to Columbus at about 5:00 this evening.

2008: Another mild and sunny day, highs in the middle 40s. Crows called between 7:30 and 8:00. Robins were chirping near the yard at about 11:00, and a cardinal sang a little later.

2009: Crows at 7:45. Early sun, then quickening clouds. Rain forecast for all day tomorrow. I looked again for the Christmas polygonia in the leaves below the crucifix: nothing.

2010: The New Year's thaw came full on today, melting almost all the snow, the sidewalks and the lawns appearing for the first time in three full weeks.

2012: When I first arrived at Gethsemani a week ago, a ladybug visited my room, flew around my lamp a while, was dead the next day. This morning, I have two new ladybugs, one sitting on the toilet seat, one climbing the light by my bed. These are the red, summer ladybugs, not the pale Asian ladybeetles. The temperature is below freezing outside. If I put them out, they will die sooner. Below my window, two mockingbirds are performing an intense randori in a tree, circling, swooping in and around the branches over and over again.

2013: Crows at 7:40 this morning. Blustery, light snow, little sound after the crows were gone.

2014: Jon Whitmore reports hearing sandhill cranes flying over just a couple of miles west of the village.

2019: Deep cold follows the long two-week warm spell, cruel wind tossing the bamboo back and forth. But this morning when the temperature was still in the 50s, the koi raced to meet me and feed. This afternoon at Ellis Pond, a great flock of geese approached, circled, and then flew over to the fields on the other side of the road. Back in town, a sizeable flock of starlings played in the trees. Downtown, a flock of robins, about three dozen, were singing their full spring song and clucking, according to Leslie.

Journal: Riding the Winter Solstice

This they tell and whether it happened so or not I do not know; but if you think about it, you can see that it is true.

Black Elk

Always in search of seasons and seeking a retreat at solstice, I spent the Christmastide at a monastery, where all the seasons are taken very seriously.

Now that I am back, people ask me what it was like to leave family and festivities for silence and solitude. I tell them that the isolation seemed to speed up psychological time and allowed me to process so many thoughts and feelings. And the more I took part in the monastic rhythm, the more I realized that I was becoming part of an elaborate and deeply layered mystery play about higher time, part of a celebration of God on Earth.

So, imagine a majestic theater in a castle, surrounded by a thousand acres of hills and lakes and woods. And imagine that a company of men – think of them as actors or monks or whatever you want to call them – puts on daily performances from 3:15 a.m. until 8:00 p.m., a total of eight each day, year around.

These performances are like acts of an immense theatrical production. The acts have names: Vigils, Lauds, Mass, Terce, Sext, None, Vigils and Compline. They are highly complex compositions that follow the seasons of the year and change with them. They are choreographed to perfection, always start and end as scheduled, include readings, songs, and prayers, and the actors chant their most important messages like some kind of Greek chorus.

Now imagine all of this, and make one adjustment to the theater analogy. These actors believe that their play is reality, and that the story they tell is true, not only historically but also existentially - so that they spend all of their lives together in community, celibate, in costume, and dedicated to that repeating seasonal drama, putting it on decade after decade, trying to perfect it and trying to live their most authentic selves.

Imagine a little more: The theater is almost always full. An audience comes from all over the country to watch as well as to become participants in some of these performances for a day or longer. Each person attends and observes and takes part in a different way, trying to understand what is happening, trying to follow the plot, taking advantage of the intermissions, which sometimes last three or four hours, to walk in the woods, to reflect and read and meditate on the story and their lives.

People wonder where I stand on all of this. Am I a partisan of this troupe's message? Do I believe their tale? And I have to admit that for me the line between a suspension of disbelief and belief itself is a very porous line, and that my identification with or love of certain characters in a book or play often crosses over into my life.

Great stories are almost always true, whether they "happened so or not." Grace is subtle. Narratives cut many ways. By the time I returned home to Yellow Springs, my questions about reality and the semblance of reality were no longer meaningful. As a spectator, I had unwittingly joined the drama, and now I practice my part.

December 31st
The 365th Day of the Year

Now I have told the year from dawn to dusk,
Its morning and its evening and its noon;
Once round the Sun our slanting orbit rolled,
Four times the season changed, thirteen the moon....

Vita Sackville-West

Sunrise/set: 7:57/5:20
Day's Length: 9 hours 23 minutes
Average High/Low: 36/21
Average Temperature: 28
Record High: 67 – 1951
Record Low: - 6 – 1976

The Daily Weather

New Year's Eve is usually cloudier than the 30th, bringing overcast conditions seven days in ten. There is a 35 percent chance of rain, ten percent for snow. Today's highs are in the 60s five percent of the years, in the 50s fifteen percent of the time, in the 40s twenty-five percent, in the 30s forty-five percent, in the 20s ten percent. Below-zero temperatures on this date are infrequent.

The Natural Calendar

Deep Winter, the coldest period of the year throughout North America, generally begins tomorrow and lasts until January 28. Sunrise reaches its latest time of the year on this date, and dawn continues to occur at that time until January 11.

The outside garden is almost always gone by now. Collards and kale, and well-mulched carrots and beets can survive to this point in season, but January's cold spells eventually take them. Indoors, however, tomato and pepper plants, seeded in middle summer and brought inside before frost, could still be producing fruit in a south window. Basil, parsley, rosemary, thyme and oregano may also continue to provide fresh seasoning. And the seeds of bedding plants sprout under lights, softening winter with their April green.

The Stars

Tonight, Orion is almost overhead at bedtime, and Gemini towers behind it. The evenings of early spring push Orion deep into the west, bring Cancer and Leo overhead, and by the time late spring reaches the 40th Parallel, Orion will have disappeared from the dark sky, and boxy Libra will be rising in the southeast, the *Corona Borealis* above it.

Daybook

1983: This past December was the third coldest ever, with an average temperature of 21.9.

1988: Crows calling all morning. Small flocks of starlings seen along Dayton-Yellow Springs Road.

1989: The world is not getting warmer here yet. This December was the coldest on record, with a 17-degree average. Then today, after two weeks of deep cold, a week of mornings below zero, and six inches of snow, the winds switched to the south. Highs went up to the 40s. When the snow melted, the garlic mustard was just as strong as it had been before this most bitter December in history. A cardinal sang loud and long at 11:41 a.m.

1991: In the Vale: a flock of robins, maybe ten birds wintering over, seen along the path. Honeysuckle berries still hold on for them.

1998: The first snow of the year overnight, maybe half an inch. In the greenhouse, two jade trees have been flowering for a couple of days now. In the garden, temperatures into the teens and single digits have finally killed the chard and broccoli. The pond's watercress has been locked in ice for almost a week now and seems dead above the water line. The cold has made the mullein, lamb's ear and feverfew droop. At Springfield, no sign of the great crow gathering.

2001: The mild autumn and early winter temperatures of 2001 gave a sample of what this region might be like under a benign wave of global warming. Averages were about five degrees above normal in November and December that year, and such warmth is more characteristic of the upper Border States than of the lower Midwest. If the earth's climate is indeed changing, the Farmland Country of 2050 might consistently enjoy a more moderate winter, something similar to an average 20th century winter in Washington DC, Louisville, Kentucky, or the Piedmont of North Carolina.

Under that climatic regimen, local turkey vultures would be staying the whole year instead of leaving at the end of October, joining the geese to further mellow our suburban habitat.

Although the leaves would still be down, falling more in response to the day's length than to extremes of cold, the vegetation in woods and fields would be showing signs of a new season, one which had surfaced only briefly in the centuries before.

Following leafdrop, the land always passes through a "second spring" in which the foliage of certain wildflowers starts growing back as though winter had already come and gone. Up until now, severe cold has always destroyed this revival or held it firmly in abeyance.

With a new seasonal order, second spring would simmer in the undergrowth then gradually push out all the way into first spring a month or two before its parallels of the mid and late 1900s. Every November would bring a complete second flowering of golden forsythia. Dandelions would always be in bloom. White clover, red clover, chickweed, bittercress, black medic, and shepherd's purse would open beside them. Purple deadnettle would spread and blossom all over the gardens. Lanky yellow sow thistles would quiver by the roadsides.

Pussy willows might be out for New Year's Eve. Crocus and daffodils would grace the middle of January. The grass would become long, dark green and lush, needing to be cut every few weeks. Emerald wheat would transform the fields, surging to its April height by the end of January. Moss would stretch to the sun on its wet logs. Caraway, Queen Anne's lace, poison hemlock, ragwort, dock, wild parsnip, and yarrow would reclaim their March territories by Groundhog Day. Autumn violets would become April violets without pause.

179

2002: A cardinal sang at 8:12 this morning, the temperature outside a gentle 50 degrees

2003: A clear and gentle New Year's Eve, sky without a cloud, temperatures expected to reach 40. This morning, Jeanie and Dianne saw about 20 more turkey vultures across from the riding center. Then they came across a small flock of robins, their breasts so bright in the rising sun that they appeared pure red. At home, I noticed one starling scouting for a nest by the southeast corner of our eaves. Cardinals were singing as I split wood a little later.

2004: Almost all the snow of the great solstice storm is gone after four days of thaw in the 40s and 50s. The river is high and strong from snowmelt. Downstream, the surface of the water is still frozen.

2006: Rain for New Year's Eve. In Washington, D.C., spring iris, aconites and snowdrops are reported in bloom after an especially warm December.

2007: A brief cardinal song heard about 10:00 this morning in the alley. A hard cold front moves in for New Year's Day. Strong gusts of wind began about 8:00 this evening; the tin roof rattled and banged.

2008: A blustery dawn, bamboo groaning and scraping against the south windows. Then sun and clouds, the wind softening. On the way to the airport with Neysa, we saw a sparrow hawk, two flocks of swooping starlings. Returning to town, we passed a small murder of crows along Dayton-Yellow Springs Road. Two large opossums had been killed along that road in the past couple of days. Now at the end of Early Winter, the honeysuckle berries are down to only a small percentage of their late November numbers. The butterfly bush leaves are drooping, finally showing the stress of the cold days; Japanese knotweed leaves are almost all down, and the oakleaf hydrangea leaves are twisted and contracting, starting to fall. All the hulls have disappeared from around the orange bittersweet berries.

2009: A dark and cloudy morning with only crows calling. Rain is forecast for this afternoon, cold for tomorrow. The sparrows feed ravenously at the back feeder, a few finches at the thistle seeds. Fog closes down the Columbus airport.

2010: Crows at 7:54 this morning. Mary Sue says that this is the first morning she hasn't seen the sandhill cranes. Mild in the 50s throughout the day, reaching 62 late in the afternoon. Robins peeping. At the Crawfords' house, Diane told how robins and starlings "whooshed" back and forth outside her workshop before Christmas. Across the lower Plains, twenty tornadoes caused havoc as the New Year's cold front moved east. From Montana, a "Poor Will" reader reported a blizzard, just as predicted.

By the end of the day, all the snow that had covered the ground throughout December, melted in a grand and wonderful thaw. The cold had lasted 28 days, the month more than six degrees below normal.

Walking around the yard, I found that some things were a little flatter than they had been in November. A few late Osage leaves, covered before I was able to rake them, were matted, sodden and dark. Celandine, lungwort, lamb's ear, parsley, and sweet rockets had all their leaves pushed akimbo. My neighbor's lily-of-the-valley foliage had been pressed to the ground by the storm on the 13th, leaf tips forced to point east by the hard west wind.

The snow had bent the New England asters and the false boneset, and now they were prostrate to seed the soil around them. The oakleaf hydrangea and knotweed leaves had taken a beating. Almost all of the honeysuckle berries had fallen, cluttering the sidewalk.

The grass was still half green, just like it had been at Thanksgiving. The precocious pussy willows that had opened a crack in October were opening a little more. The lamium and the mint were standing tall and strong. The hellebores near our south property line had risen back to their autumn height.

Creeping Charlie was ruddy but creeping. Japanese honeysuckle and winterberries had been darkened by temperatures near zero, but were still firm. Chickweed was bright between the bricks in the outdoor patio. Pachysandra was upright and budded. Garlic mustard had not been touched by all the cold, stood defiantly against mustard pullers of April. Blood-red peony buds still crouched

181

in the peony garden. Waterleaf peered out from the mulch.

2012: Gethsemani to Yellow Springs: Two murmurations of starlings seen. An inch or so of snow on the ground all the way from western Kentucky through southwestern Ohio.

2013: Crows late this cloudy, snowy morning: 8:05.

2014: Scott reported sighting of sandhill cranes about 5:00 p.m.

2015: Flurried and wind. Betty Ross called to say she had seen a sizeable pod of 36 cranes flying over the covered bridge and the southern part of Glen Helen at about 1:45 in the afternoon.

2016: John Blakelock called around noon: He was hearing cranes over his house.

2017: Wild cherry fruits have fallen in the snow along Limestone Street this morning, the cherries maybe two-thirds down. Supermoon waxing to 97 percent full today, approaching perigee, light snow steady, even deeper cold moving in, below-zero lows in the forecast for the next six days, just right for cranes: Karen Blevins called from Smith Road off of Dayton-Yellow Springs Road: "We saw three sandhill cranes today in the cornfield just by themselves, but they were there!" Casey reported seeing maybe forty or fifty this afternoon, and Jill thought she heard them.

And Liz wrote: "Another migration of the sandhills and I missed them again—maybe next time. Meanwhile, the morning was graced by a mature yellow bellied sapsucker who spent much time with the suet and also on the tree. I wonder if it's the juvenile all grown up which I originally saw in 2014? I don't know if they are unusual around here, but they are always an exciting visitor in my yard."

2018: Rain throughout the Middle Atlantic and the East, a high in Yellow Springs of 62 degrees. From Fontanelli, Italy, Ivano sends a photo of a large, red and blue and gold *Aglais io* butterfly he found on the woodpile.

2019: Hard wind (to 40 mph) and light sleet. This morning a small flock of robins, maybe a dozen in all, took turns drinking from a seed flat full of water near my studio window. All the geese, about 300, had gathered on Ellis Pond, indifferent to the wind and cold. Leslie reported that she counted 14 robins drinking from her patio pond, and dozens of starlings, too. Are the starlings and the robins both coming together in town earlier?

2019: The Year in Review
January, February, March

In spite of dire forecasts about climate change for the decade to come, there is some security in the stability of the recent local seasons. This year has been unexceptional in many ways; its trajectory has followed that of most years in decades past, and it can serve as an example of what normal is like in Yellow Springs and most of southwestern Ohio at the beginning of the 21st century.

Chickadees and titmice greeted the new year with their early mating calls, unfazed, it seemed, by Winter Storm Gaia that brought nine inches of snow on the 12th. Emily saw a bald eagle on the 15th. Louise saw bluebirds on the 18th, Kat saw them on the 27th. Cardinals began their consistent pre-dawn calls on the 28th, the same day that a skunk sprayed Jill's garage.

Record cold of minus 8 degrees closed the month, but doves and song sparrows were singing by February 4. Sap was running at the Flying Mouse Farm on the 13th. Robins that had spent the winter scattered throughout the Glen and the village, came together in large flocks. The geese of Ellis Pond, their numbers reaching close to 300, were pairing up by the middle of the month. Casey called in the first red-winged blackbird's arrival on the 22nd, and the 25th brought beds of yellow aconites to bloom around town.

Leslie reported the first blush of gold on the gold finches at her feeder on March 2. Songbirds were pairing up by the 10th. Spring peepers were peeping by the 14th. No longer inhibited by the morning darkness, robins began their morning chorus on March 16. The first honeybees visited the crocuses on the 19th. The first daffodil finally opened on March 29, two days after the first butterfly sighting (a mourning cloak) and the beginning of wildflower time throughout the Glen

April, May, June

The rainfall for March was almost four inches above normal, and there was no chance for farmlands around Yellow Springs to be ready for planting at the arrival of Middle Spring. Temperatures, however, were a few degrees above average, and golden forsythia and daffodils greeted the gilding goldfinches on schedule. Frogs and grass snakes, bumblebees, ticks and red admiral butterflies appeared in the first week of the moth. Violets, dandelions, fruit trees all flowered together at midmonth. Villagers reported morel mushrooms on the 27th, the first hummingbird on the 29th.

May's temperatures followed April's gentle lead. Petal fall began with the arrival of Baltimore Orioles on the 1st. Spring rains continued, however, and golden tall groundsel filled the unplanted fields. On May 10, the cascades thundered with tons on runoff and parts of the Glen were flooded. The farm calendar was delayed, but not the typical sequence for insects, plants and animals. Maple seeds were falling by the 13th. On May 14, bees were swarming at Dennie's. Butterflies were relatively common: red admirals, sulphurs, skippers. Locusts and clovers bloomed in the month's third week. Tree frogs called in the woods beyond Ellis Pond. On the 24th, Matt saw the first firefly, a couple of days early. Songbirds filled the Glen, the annual count only slightly lower than the year before.

The tornado of May 27 was the major anomalous event of the month. Was it a sign that "Tornado Alley" has moved closer to Yellow Springs? Only the years ahead will tell.

But June kept to June's schedule. Mulberries were ripe by the 1st. Fledglings left the nests to eat them. Hostas and roses and lilies bloomed on time. Relishing the rains, fireflies were abundant. Lesile saw the first raccoon kit on June 6. Don's pie cherries were ripe by June 8. Hackberry butterflies and monarchs appeared by the 11th, Japanese beetles on the 23rd, chiggers on the 28th. The first cicadas called on the 30th. Most of the fields around Yellow Springs were sprouting with corn and soybeans by the end of the month, and they grew lush and tall throughout the rest of the summer.

July, August, September

Heat and drought followed the wet early spring. May was four degrees above average, June slightly below, July almost five degrees above average, August about two degrees above average, September eight degrees above average (the warmest ever recorded here, with records set on the 27th, 28th and 30th).

The last weeks of July and all of August brought only half the normal rainfall, and September brought just half an inch (as opposed to an average of three and a half inches).

Temperatures and precipitation were challenging to farmers and gardeners, and many trees and plants showed signs of stress as autumn approached. Still, most of the fauna and flora followed their schedule of the past half century.

Cicadas sang from the end of June into October. Katydids began to call in the ending on schedule July 20. Tree frogs, tree crickets and field crickets were loud from late July toward frost. Monarch butterflies were plentiful in some areas, and a variety of butterflies graced village gardens throughout the summer. Spiders, however, seemed less abundant, daddy longlegs were sparse in the undergrowth, and relatively few large Orb-weavers constructed their webs in the area.

Fledgling birds were abundant throughout the summer, and flocking began by the middle of July, the first starling murmuration sighted on July 15. The first geese formation passed over town on August 2, and by September 25 a small flock had gathered across from Ellis Pond, the first gathering of the new year. Grackles flocked to Leslie's property on September 10, the same day that nighthawks few over the village.

October, November, December

The first three days of October brought unusual heat in the 90s, and the month, overall, was five degrees above normal. In the midst of summer-like temperatures, the markers of fall were welcome but unremarkable: the frequent murmurations (swooping flocks) of starlings, the chanting of tree frogs, tree crickets and katydids in the warmest nights, the shedding of black walnuts, acorns, hickory nuts, pecans. Frost put an end to most insect song on the 12th, and leafturn began then, peaking pretty much on schedule around the 25th. The local harvest of corn and soybeans was complete by the end of the month, although with yields below average. One unusual occurrence, according to an observer: yellow jackets and ants failed to visit his hummingbird feeder after the hummingbirds departed, something that hadn't happened before.

Balancing the heat of October, November was four degrees below average. Ginkgo and white mulberry trees shed their leaves in the nights of November 7 and 8. The first significant snowfall, three inches, fell on the 12th, punctuated by Betty's sighting of the first sandhill cranes of the season that afternoon. Robins, which had remained silent through much of the dry late summer and autumn began their winter intermittent cheeping, and the number of geese around Ellis Pond swelled to more than a hundred.

December was mild, the Christmas cold front failing to arrive. Ellis Pond froze then thawed. More geese gathered in the fields. The sandhill cranes came though on December 6, witnessed by Jon and Betty. More cranes flew over on the 15th, seen by John, Casey, Jim, Anne, Audrey and Cliff, and more cranes on the 18th, reported by Anne and Betty and Mike, more on the 23rd by Emily. Megan saw a bald eagle on the 16th, adding to the slowly growing list of sightings in our area. At the end of the month, small flocks of overwintering robins visited local ponds, and starlings clustered in the village.

Few unusual events seem to have occurred in the natural flow of this year, and it appears that the local fauna and flora are keeping within the template of decades past. Still, nine out of the last twelve months have brought above-average temperatures, as well as extended periods of both rainfall and drought, to Yellow Springs. Information from around the globe suggests that climate change will have unexpected consequences and that southwestern Ohio will experience significant environmental events in the decades ahead. We may soon need to yield, as Wendell Berry has said, "to the condition that what we have expected is not there."

2020: An inch of snow overnight, the New Year's Eve low-pressure system arriving a day early, the barometer rising and highs only near freezing today. Tat in Madison, Wisconsin, got eight inches of snow on the 29th, John in Lincoln, Nebraska, six inches the 28th. Average temperature for the month was 35 degrees, about four degrees above normal. Precipitation was an inch, two below normal, with about six inches total snowfall.

The Year in Review: 2020

The year began above normal, January's temperatures more than eight degrees over the typical 28. Ed's snowdrops were open on January 1, and Lenten roses were budding in my dooryard by the 7th. The temperature reached a record 67 degrees on January 11th. Maple sap was flowing at the Flying Mouse Farm on the 29th, and Audrey reported golden aconites in bloom at Winter and Dayton Streets on the 30th.

February followed suit, two and a half degrees above average. Honeybees were out on the 3rd. Casey saw bluebirds on the 4th, and starlings and red-winged blackbirds came to town by the middle of the month, around the time the great flock of Canadian geese left Ellis Pond in pairs.

March was warm as well, six degrees above normal, and the progress of the vegetation reflected the warmth. Forsythia bloomed on the 13th, crab apples leafed a week to 10 days ahead of schedule. As in 2019, rainfall was plentiful, and planting of many fields took place later than usual. Heavy rains brought flooding to the Glen and magnificent torrents at the Cascades.

April and May reversed the warming trend, each a degree below normal, bringing blooming dates back closer to average, much like they were in the 1980s. Baltimore orioles arrived on schedule in the first week of May. Aida called to report the arrival of cedar waxwings at the end of the month, an annual event of late May. Grackles were depositing fecal sacks in ponds during June's first week. Three bald eagles were sighted in the area during the year.

June returned the year's temperature to above normal, and Yellow Springs remained warm throughout the remainder of the year. Many insects were plentiful in the benign weather. Field crickets sang by the 6th. Tree crickets were buzzing by mid month. Blue-bodied dragon flies hunted along the shores of Ellis Pond. Cicadas and katydids called on schedule. Fireflies were abundant in the village, although not in other places in Ohio. But butterflies were scarce, and, for the third year in a row, autumn's orb weaver spiders failed to weave their giant webs.

Peak leaf color occurred at the normal time, between October 16 and 22, as the geese started to return to Ellis Pond. A killing frost occurred on November 2, but November ended five degrees above normal, the highest since 1975. An unusual warm spell occurred during the second week, with a record 80 on November 8 and another record, 78, on November 10. December was four degrees above average, with a brief heat wave between the 9th and 11th. Sandhill cranes appeared between ridges of high barometric pressure on December 4, 22, 24, 25 and 26.

The European Union's Copernicus Climate Change Service reported that 2020 had tied with 2016 as the warmest year for the planet. In the Dayton area, the year's average temperature was 55 degrees, not the warmest in history (the warmest year being 56.1 in 1921) but well above the normal of around 52. Even so, zeitgebers (markers in nature that tell the time of year) seemed to occur pretty much as they always have. When I compared my daybook entries from the early 1980s to those of 2020, I could see relatively few changes.

One disheartening exception was a significant decline the frequency and variety of insects. My backyard notes for this past summer reflect the dramatic state-wide decline of butterflies, almost 30 percent over the average numbers during the past 20 years.

According to Jerome Wiedmann of the Ohio Lepidopterist Society, "Last year and 2018 were bad years for butterflies but even by comparison to 2018 and 2019, 2020 was a very bad year for butterflies in Ohio.

"Only an average of 31 species were seen in the 2020 counts compared to a historic average of 36 species. The total number of butterflies seen (by our observers) in 2020 was only

11,308 compared to an average of 16,858 per year."

These statistics dovetail with and support the findings of studies made in Europe and North America that suggest that butterfly disappearance parallels that of insects, in general, at the rate of about two percent per year. Declines in Monarch butterfly populations have occurred even more rapidly than the butterfly population over all, a rate of seven percent per year. Since butterflies are among the most monitored species, scientists believe they are the canary in the ecological coal mine for other insects.

Recent literature suggests that global warming, habitat deterioration, pesticides and other forms of pollution all contribute to defaunation, the die-off of species. No solutions to any of these problems are likely in the near future. The math, however, is not too complex. Even a best-case scenario: fifty years times two percent equals no butterflies by 2070 (probably much sooner), except perhaps in hothouse environments where they could be raised as exotic remnants of pre-Anthropocene beauty.

For it is only at the scale of our direct, sensory interactions with the land around us that we can appropriately notice and respond to the immediate needs of the living world.

David Abram

A Compilation of Sandhill Crane Sightings: 2003 – 2020

The following are dates and observers of crane sightings near and around Yellow Springs since Rick first reported seeing them over Xenia Avenue in 2003. This listing is the natural history of crane passage through this small corner of the Lower Midwest for the dates indicated. These sightings may reflect a change in migration patterns from previous decades, but when the flyovers actually began is unknown.

November 7, 2017: Jon
November 12, 2019: Betty.
November 19, 2011: Liz
November 20, 2011: Jenny
November 21, 2014: Casey and Dianne
November 23, 2006: Liz
November 23, 2012: Liz
November 25, 2018: John and Emily
November 27, 2013: Mary
November 27, 2018: Casey and Betty
November 28, 2005: A woman on Grinnell Circle
November 28, 2012: Lori and Jill
November 30, 2007: Dorothy and Chris
November 30, 2011: Kathryn
November 30, 2020: Doug
December 1, 2011: Nick
December 2, 2003: Rick D.
December 2, 2020: Doug
December 4, 2007: Casey
December 4, 2020: Liz and Jenny and Lori
December 5, 2010: Casey and Liz
December 6, 2011: Rick and Mary D.
December 6, 2019: Betty and Jon
December 7, 2008: Casey
December 7: 2010: Casey
December 7, 2013: Ruth
December 7, 2018: Anne and Aida
December 8: 2012: Patricia
December 9, 2007: John and Ed
December 9, 2016: Doug

December 10, 2009: John
December 10, 2016: Moya
December 11, 2009: Kathryn and Aida
December 11: 2011: John
December 11: 2014: John
December 12: 2014: John
December 12, 2009: Jeanie, Casey, Ruth and Matt
December 12, 2016: Jon
December 12, 2017: Jon, Ben, Betty, Rick, John B., Maureen, Paul, Anne, Bettina
December 13, 2009: John
December 13, 2018: Lisa
December 14, 2016: Rick W.
December 14, 2017: Laura, Casey
December 15, 2016: Ed
December 15, 2019: John, Casey, Jim, Anne, Audrey, and Cliff's friend on Larken Rd.
December 16, 2009: John
December 17, 2013: Bill
December 17, 2016: Jon, Caroline
December 18, 2009: Jenny
December 18, 2016: John, Tim
December 18, 2019: Anne, Betty
December 19, 2015: John, Kurt, Mary Sue, Lori, Bob and Audrey
December 22, 2013: Mary Sue
December 22, 2017: Amy
December 22, 2017: Lin
December 22, 2020: Liz, John, Megan and Audrey
December 23, 2019: Emily
December 24, 2020: Casey, Anne, Ed, Liz and Rick
December 25, 2020: Casey, Audrey, Grant, Bill and Jill
December 26, 2020: John, Marianne, Pam, Audrey, Grant, Bill and Betty
December 28, 2011: Ruth
December 28, 2017: John
December 30, 2014: John
December 31, 2014: Scott
December 31, 2015: Betty
December 31, 2016: John

December 31, 2017: Karen, Casey, Jill
January 1, 2013: Bill
January 1, 2014: Bill, John, Michele
January 1, 2017: Jill
January 2, 2012: Jeanie, Suzanne, John
January 3, 2011: Jenny, Lauren, Kitty
January 3, 2016: John, Sue, Bob, Carol
January 4, 2017: Bob
January 6, 2018: Amy
January 10, 2016: Dennie
January 11, 2018: Mike
January 15, 2011: Liz, Peter, Mary Sue
January 17, 2016: Dennie
January 22, 2014: John and Lisa
January 26, 2015: John
February 15, 2019: John R.
February 22, 2014: John
February 23, 2014: Audrey
February 26: Emily (in Indianapolis)
February 27, 2011: Liz
March 1, 2014: Kit

Valediction for the Year

The most difficult thing for me in winter
is to stay where I am
and to keep from looking ahead into spring.
It is hard to hold steady,
to accept the bare tangle of branches,
the soft secrecy of buds,
the sleek cones of catkins
that perfectly contain both birth and death.
It is hard to remain in place
in the certainty of these things here and now:
the cold river, the crisp wind, the gray, finite sky,
the everlasting bouquets of spent flowers,
the darkening hulls of black walnuts
and Osage fruits,
the settling leaves, the low sun,
Orion in the night,
the mornings without birdsong,
the falling seeds of the winterberry,
the withering bittersweet
and honeysuckle berries,
not seeing past the horizon,
not finding God-to-come,
free from the need for summer,
self-sufficient, knowing that the center
is here as well as there
in this tight and impeccable close,
as well as in the far green paradise of June.

Bill Felker

Bill Felker has been writing almanacs and nature columns for newspapers and magazines since 1984, and he has published an annual *Poor Will's Almanack* since 2003. His radio version of *Poor Will* is broadcast weekly on WYSO, a National Public Radio station, and it is available on podcast at **www.wyso.org.** His book of essays, *Home is the Prime Meridian: Essays in Search of Time and Place and Spirit,* and the entire twelve volumes of *A Daybook for the Year in Yellow Springs, Ohio,* are available at online bookshops and Bill's website: **www.poorwillsalmanack.com**

Made in the USA
Columbia, SC
16 July 2021